LOCOMOTION PAPERS

The
Westerham Valley Railway

by
David Gould

THE OAKWOOD PRESS

© Oakwood Press & David Gould 1999

First Edition published 1974
Second Revised Edition published 1999
British Library Cataloguing in Publication Data
A Record for this book is available from the British Library
ISBN 0 85361 515 2

Typeset by Oakwood Graphics.
Repro by Ford Graphics, Ringwood, Hants.
Printed by Alpha Print (Oxford), Witney, Oxon.

A Westerham train which has just left Dunton Green: class 'F1' 4-4-0 No. A451 of Tonbridge with ex-SE&CR six-wheeled brake van and ex-LBSCR bogie Composite in about 1931. *L.T. Catchpole*

Title page: A Westerham to Dunton Green train passing through Combe Bank Wood between Brasted and Chevening Halt on 29th April, 1956. (Class 'H' No. 31164 with Set 481.) *Alan Snowdon*

Published by
The Oakwood Press
P.O. Box 13, Usk, Mon., NP5 1YS.

Contents

Prologue 5

Acknowledgements 6

Chapter One   **Westerham Before the Railway** 7

Chapter Two   **The Westerham Valley Railway Co.** 9

Chapter Three   **The Line Described** 19

Chapter Four   **South Eastern Railway** 41

Chapter Five   **South Eastern & Chatham Railway** 47

Chapter Six   **Southern Railway - 1923 to 1939** 61

Chapter Seven   **Southern Railway - 1939 to 1947** 85

Chapter Eight   **British Railways, Southern Region** 95

Chapter Nine   **Efforts to Reopen the Line** 117

Epilogue 127

Index 128

Class 'H' No. 31263 (the only member of its class still in existence) propelled a push-and-pull set converted from SR corridor stock out of Chevening Halt on 23rd September, 1961; the train was the 3.23 pm from Westerham.   *James Aston*

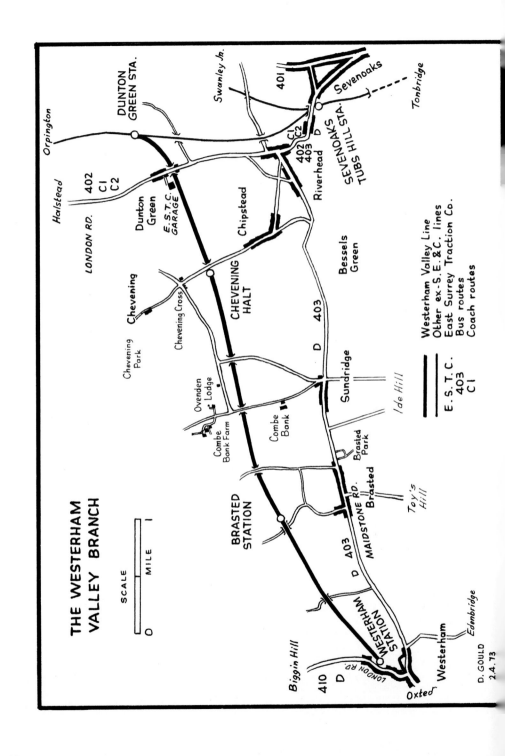

THE WESTERHAM VALLEY BRANCH

SCALE

0   MILE   1

| Westerham Valley Line |
| Other ex-S.E. & C. lines |
| East Surrey Traction Co. |
| Bus routes |
| Coach routes |

E. S. T. C.   403
C1

Orpington

Halstead

LONDON RD.   402
C1
C2

DUNTON GREEN STA.

Swanley Jn.

401

Sevenoaks

Tonbridge

Dunton Green

E.S.T.C. GARAGE

C1
C2

402
403

D

Riverhead

SEVENOAKS TUBS HILL STA.

Chipstead

Chevening

Chevening Park

Chevening Cross

CHEVENING HALT

Bessels Green

Ovenden Lodge

Combe Bank Farm

Combe Bank

D   403

Sundridge

Ide Hill

BRASTED STATION

Brasted Park

Toy's Hill

D   403

MAIDSTONE RD.

Brasted

Biggin Hill

410
D

LONDON RD.

WESTERHAM STATION

Westerham

Oxted

Edenbridge

D. GOULD
2.4.73

Prologue

By April 1961 I had been aware, for some while, of the existence of a branch line that ran to the market town of Westerham, since it was clearly shown on Bartholomew's Half-Inch Map of Kent. It was the Westerham Valley Railway, about which I, as a 14-year-old, knew absolutely nothing; although Westerham was no great distance from where I then lived I had never visited the station.

So, on a Sunday in the latter half of April 1961, I cycled to Westerham from Lingfield by way of Oxted and Limpsfield, full of the sense of wonder at the prospect of discovering something new: and the station was not going to reveal its secrets until the last minute because northward from the centre of Westerham the London Road is twisty and the station was not visible until one was almost upon it. What a delightful station it turned out to be! I was enchanted by it. The timber weatherboarded structures, including the station building, the goods shed and the tiny signal cabin; the simple track layout, with only seven sets of points; all made up a perfect little terminus very suitable as the basis of a model. I sat down in the goods yard - which was quite open and accessible - and sketched the station buildings. On that first Sunday, while I worked, class 'H' 0-4-4 tank locomotive No. 31500 and push-and-pull set No. 610 (which had been converted from Southern Railway main-line corridor stock) arrived and departed. If there was anyone on duty at the station he raised no objection to my being in the goods yard.

Having seen the line's closure date announced as Monday 30th October, 1961, and, thinking that that would be the last date of operation, I turned up at Westerham on the previous day expecting to find trains running. None appeared, and it became clear that the last day of operation had actually been Saturday 28th; I was a day late, not a day early! Not only was I unaware that the branch had no Sunday service during the winter, but also that official closure dates referred to the first day of no service, not the last day that trains ran.

In summer 1962 the Westerham Railway Association leased Westerham station from British Railways and every Sunday the station was open to the public, a penny ticket admitting the holder to the platform and waiting room, where photographs of the line were displayed. Considerably interested in what was going on, and tempted by the initial subscription rate of 2s. 6d., I decided to become a member and, on subsequent visits, was able to assist in some of the work under the guidance of Alan Snowdon - who was in charge of volunteers, most of whom were teenagers. I had a spell assisting with the repainting of the station building, the new colours being cream with maroon trim, stated to have been the colours used by the South Eastern & Chatham Railway and which looked most attractive. In the end it was all for nothing, and a line that seemed to have so much did not reopen, despite the best efforts of the Association and its hard-working committee.

Acknowledgements

For their assistance during the preparation of this book I gratefully acknowledge Messrs James Aston, Thomas Burnham, Denis Cullum, Roy Edwards, R.W. Kidner, R.C. Riley and Alan Snowdon. Tom in particular has sent me copious notes about the line and, having read my manuscript, also made many helpful suggestions about how it could be improved! Several obscure points have been clarified by Mr Kidner, whose many years of studying the Southern Railway have left him with a deep knowledge of the subject. Roy Edwards and Alan Snowdon were happy to speak about their time on the committee of the Westerham Valley Railway Association and supplied some 'inside information'.

In many cases the source reference, if a book or journal, is quoted within the text. Descriptions of train services, engine and carriage workings come from the various official documents produced by the railway and are mainly in private hands. Minute books and other timetables are to be found in the British Transport Historical Records collection, now at Kew. Those used include

SER1/44 to SER1/48	Board Minute Books, 11.1875 to 10.1883
SEC1/85, SEC1/89	General Purposes Sub-Committee Minutes, 1902/3, 1906/7
WMV1	Westerham Valley Railway General Meeting Minute Book
PYB1/737A	House of Commons - Westerham Valley Railway Bill Session 1876
MT6 300/11	Board of Trade inspection report, 1881
TT26/48	South Eastern Railway Service Timetable, 1883
TT12	SE&CR Service Timetables, various years
TT20	Southern Railway Working Timetables, various years

I should like to dedicate this book to the memory of the promoters of the Westerham Valley Railway Company and to the all the committee members of the ill-fated Westerham Valley Railway Association.

David Gould
East Grinstead
1999

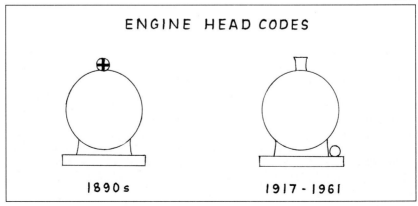

ENGINE HEAD CODES

1890s   1917 - 1961

Chapter One

Westerham Before the Railway

Westerham, a small and delightful town situated - as its name implies - at the western extremity of Kent, is mentioned in the Domesday survey of 1086; 'Comes Eustachius ten de rege Oistreham. Goduin tenuit de rege E (Count Eustace holds Westerham for the King. Earl Godwin held it for King Edward the Confessor).' There were 42 villagers with seven smallholders and 10 slaves.

St Mary's Church, whose fabric includes 13th, 14th and 15th century work, with walls of rubble sandstone, was altered in 1854 and 'restored' during 1882/3. It features a shingled spire.

The town, which in 1227 was permitted to hold a market every Wednesday, is built on the lower slopes of the Greensand Ridge which rises to some 800 ft at Toys Hill to the south. To the north the chalk escarpment of the North Downs reaches over 800 ft at Westerham Hill. Between them lies the Vale of Holmesdale, which is formed of the Gault Clay, an unstable material on which there has been little building because of its tendency to disrupt foundations; and this instability was to create problems for the railway builders. Through the Vale of Holmesdale runs the Darent River, which rises in Squerryes Park.

'Squerryes' appears to be derived from 'squirrels', and the de Squerie took their name from the estate. They died out in 1463. A red-brick mansion, Squerryes Court, was built between 1680 and 1686 by Sir Nicholas Crispe, and in 1731 it was purchased by John Warde ('the father of fox-hunting') from the Earl of Jersey. By 1876 the owner was Lt-Col C. Warde, who was to be instrumental in getting a branch railway built to Westerham.

Westerham's most famous son is James Wolfe, hero of Quebec. He was born at the vicarage on 2nd January, 1727, but grew up in a 17th century house called 'Spiers'. A friend of John Warde, he received his commission in the grounds of Squerryes Court in 1741, and at Quebec his comrade-in-arms was George Warde, the youngest son of John. General Wolfe died on 13th September, 1759, but it was not until 150 years later that a statue of him was erected by the Royal Colonial Institute on Westerham Green, being unveiled on 6th January, 1911 by Field Marshall Lord Roberts. 'Spiers' had been renamed Quebec House in honour of the event, and in 1918 was given to the National Trust

The population of Westerham in 1801 was 1,344 and by 1876 it had risen to 1,770. James Thorne, in his *Handbook to the Environs of London* (1876), describes Westerham as a small market town, pleasantly situated in Holmesdale near the source of the River Darent; 'a long straggling place, roomy for its population, and the houses far from crowded; rural, quiet, perhaps a little dull'. There had been some westward extension of the town, a new public hall had been built, the shops improved and there was a cottage hospital. In 1874 the Moreton Almshouses, in London Road, were built using timber framing and sandstone. There were two inns: the 19th century King's Arms, a 'good house' where the Wednesday market was held; and the much older George and Dragon on the other side of the High Street.

Also on the Godstone to Sevenoaks road, 1½ miles east of Westerham, was the village of Brasted (earlier spelling, Brastead) whose name is pronounced with a long 'a'. Thorne in 1876 says it was a pleasant rural village on the right bank of the Darent, surrounded by hop-gardens, parks and woodlands. The wide main street featured well-spaced cottages, old and new, and by the gates of Brasted Park (owned by Squire William Tipping) was the White Hart, 'a modern antique'.

William Tipping, born near Liverpool in 1816, had watched the Liverpool & Manchester Railway being built; he never lost his enthusiasm for railways and by 1876 had become a Director of 13 railway companies, including the London & North Western (LNWR), the North London and the Danube & Black Sea. After spending some time in France he had purchased Brasted Park for £20,000 in 1853 and soon became very popular with the local people. He was Member of Parliament for Stockport from 1868 to 1874.

Transport communication in the Vale of Holmesdale at this time was poor. The nearest railway stations to Westerham were Edenbridge, four miles to the south on the Redhill to Tonbridge line, and Sevenoaks, five miles to the east.

The South Eastern Railway (SER) had opened its new main line from Chislehurst to Sevenoaks via Orpington and Dunton Green on 2nd March, 1868, and extended it to Tonbridge on 1st June, 1868. It had obtained an Act of Parliament on 23rd July, 1864 (27 and 28 Vict. cap. 98), authorising it to construct a branch line to Westerham, with a capital of £70,000 in shares and £23,000 on loan, but nothing had been done. The powers were renewed in 1867 and 1870 again without result.

It was William Tipping who in 1870 successfully persuaded the SER to abandon its 1864 powers, with the result that although the SER's Act of 2nd August, 1870, gave an extension of time plus powers to allow local enterprise to build the line if desired there was no further action. The SER was not very anxious to commit itself to building a line and so did not take much 'persuading' to leave things be, but for a time Squire Tipping earned the opprobium of certain local residents.

And now it was 1875 and Westerham was still without a railway; but despite the many disappointments of the last few years the town had not lost heart. It wanted a railway and somehow it would have one.

Chapter Two

The Westerham Valley Railway Company

Well aware of the advantages that rail communication would bring to the town and the surroundings (there were nurseries, breweries, maltings, general agriculture and hop-growing), and tired of waiting for the SER to make a move, several local worthies formed a company to build a line itself. Among those behind it were Joseph Kitchin, a hop grower and farmer; Richard Durtnell, owner of a long-established building firm in Rectory Lane, Brasted; E. Dye, Royal Farmers' Insurance agent; W. Fox; and Dr Charles Robert Thompson. One of the chief promoters, William Tipping, of Brasted Park, had underwritten a sizeable part of the sum of £50,000 to enable the Parliamentary Bill to be promoted.

The description of the proposed line was similar in most respects to that of the South Eastern's original Act of 1864: Railway No. 1, 4 miles 45 chains long, was to run from Dunton Green, in the parish of Otford, via Brasted to Westerham, and Railway No. 2, 3 miles 70 chains long, from Westerham to Oxted, where it would terminate.

William Tipping's change of face seems odd, but perhaps he had felt that he could not become personally prominent when associated with an SER branch but with a locally-promoted line he could; and as a Director of the LNWR he was confident that the SER would afford him the respect he felt due to him. That he was not in the least in awe of Sir Edward Watkin, whom he clearly regarded as his equal, is apparent from this forthright and bluntly-expressed letter sent to the SER Chairman on 17th November, 1875.

Brasted Park,
17th November, 1875

Dear Sir Edward,

You are of course aware that Westerham is agog upon a new branch of which Mr Grover the Engineer is the moving power. Sufficient money has been subscribed for Parliamentary purposes next Session, and 'tis said that the Brighton favour and the South Eastern is inclined to look kindly. They have been to me from the beginning, but not knowing your *real* policy, and having pulled with your Co. in the previous Westerham Bill, and being a Director here, I have declined giving my name or helping in any way.

Have the goodness to tell me privately your 'diplomatic incline' - are you assenting or opposing?

Of course it will not be wise to play the dog in the manger in the district - that is to say, if you won't or can't help Westerham you must not use your power to prevent it helping itself, but inasmuch as you gave me your word to do your [utmost] possible to serve Westerham I shall not support or assist what you oppose, and as a rule a scheming Engineer always sells a district.

Very truly yours,
W. Tipping

When this letter was read at the SER Board meeting on 18th November it seems to have been received in stunned silence; at least, no comments or decisions as to what action to take are recorded. The Directors would have known that Watkin was not accustomed to being dictated to - he was the one who usually did the dictating.

On 2nd February, 1876, a deputation from Westerham met representatives of the South Eastern and London, Brighton & South Coast Boards, and the SER must have then decided to oppose the Westerham - Oxted part of the scheme. Watkin, the Hon. James Byng (Deputy Chairman) and E.H. Knatchbull-Hugessen, MP, were appointed to draw up an agreement between the SER and the Westerham Valley Railway Co. (WVR) regarding the proposed line from Dunton Green to Westerham. Watkin and Tipping met on 24th February to arrange for the working of the line 'after its efficient construction on the principle of a percentage proportion with a reasonable and moderate minimum'; but, despite these apparently friendly relations, the SER still felt the necessity of asserting itself by its announced intention to petition against the Bill in Parliament 'to secure the Company's interest'. If the WVR withdrew the Oxted proposal the SER would automatically withdraw its opposition.

So, at the House of Commons Session of 22nd March, 1876 (Westerham Valley Railway Bill), the promoters put their case for obtaining an Act of Parliament authorising construction of a railway. At the start of the Session the terms were laid down: that the promoters withdraw Railway No. 2, and that the South Eastern Railway undertook to provide plant, rolling stock and to work and maintain Railway No. 1 at 50 per cent of the gross receipts. The SER, who had already guaranteed the Westerham Valley Railway a minimum toll of £2,500 a year, could purchase the line on six months' notice at a premium of £10 per cent on the capital expended.

Joseph Kitchin was asked if Westerham really needed a railway, since there was already an omnibus, and he declared it took three hours to do the five-mile journey between Westerham and Sevenoaks. 'They stop at every public house on the road,' he said. The twice-daily horse bus carried about 15 passengers ; sometimes it was so crowded that people were left behind.

The Engineer, John William Grover, of 9 Victoria Chambers, Westminster, was asked to give details of the proposed line. He stated that Railway No. 1, Dunton Green to Westerham, was 4 miles 45 chains long, he would take sufficient land for a double line, his worst gradient was 1 in 70 and his worst curve 18 chains radius, and that his estimate of the cost was £46,358. The land to be taken was wet and marshy, and so presumably of little use to farmers.

The only landowner to oppose the scheme, William John Tonge, was at the 1876 Session to put *his* case. He had not opposed the 1864 Bill and, when asked why not, he maintained that he did not reckon to oppose big railway companies. He owned Chipstead Place and some land about a mile from Dunton Green, and complained that its beauty would be spoilt because the railway would sever it right in two.

But despite Mr Tonge, the Bill went through the various stages, although with the expected modification: that the line be made only to Westerham and not to Oxted, Railway No. 2 being struck out.

On 24th July, 1876, the Westerham Valley Railway Company was incorporated by Act of Parliament, 39-40 Vict. cap. 166.

In the months that followed the lengthy business of negotiations between the WVR and the landowners took place, with much correspondence and tentative agreements between the various parties, although no land was actually purchased until 1879. In February 1877 the WVR decided that the South Eastern's guarantee of £2,500 per annum was not enough and asked the Board to increase it to £2,750 so that 'the capital could then be provided and the line made without delay'. A month later the SER agreed to do this, and by November 1877 the company's law clerk, who had been in touch with the WVR's solicitor, had satisfied himself that the land could be acquired for the sum named by the Westerham company, although he was curious to know what would be the cost of building the line. Francis Brady, the South Eastern's Engineer, was ordered to examine the plans, and in February 1878 Lucas & Aird sent in an estimate of £63,965 for building the line, although this was not taken up.

After a year's delay - entirely caused by the WVR - -the formal agreement between that company and the South Eastern was approved at a special meeting of the shareholders at London Bridge on 4th April, 1878.

The complete lack of progress made by the Westerham Valley suggests that funds were insufficient, presumably because the company had failed to sell enough shares. Some were sold to the contractor (a not uncommon practice which sometimes led to the bankruptcy of railway contractors) and there was still not enough money to pay the landowners, so the company had to go to the South Eastern for money. Another agreement had therefore to be drawn up, and it was to be mid-1879 before things would really begin to move. The Westerham Valley Railway Company would still exist but would now be totally dependent on the South Eastern. Possibly Watkin felt that with the London, Chatham & Dover on the east, quite capable of supporting a scheme for a line from Otford to Westerham, and the London, Brighton & South Coast on the west, it was well worth the money to occupy the Vale of Holmesdale.

In May 1878 Sir Edward Watkin and the Hon. James Byng were appointed the South Eastern's representatives on the Board of the WVR Co. Byng resigned as a Director of the WVR in July 1879, being replaced by the Rt Hon. E.H. Knatchbull-Hugessen, MP. Charles Sheath was appointed Secretary of the WVR at the end of May 1878.

Next, the SER needed to purchase the WVR's Act of Parliament and take over all agreements made with local landowners. Work on building the junction at Dunton Green was planned to start towards the end of 1878, but actually nothing was done until October 1879. Negotiations to purchase land for the branch began late in 1878, and the SER Directors saw no reason why the line should not be built by 1880 - but it took a while longer.

Apparently little progress in land purchase had been made by May 1879, and as the statutory time allowed for doing so was due to expire in July Watkin and Byng sought the authority of the SER Board to assist the WVR. This was given. It seems there was some sort of dispute between the Engineer of the WVR, John Grover, and the SER's Engineer, Francis Brady (who was responsible for the works at Dunton Green); and so William Tipping, with his London & North Western connections, decided to seek the advice of Stephenson, the LNWR's Engineer. In June 1879 the SER subscribed some capital in advance for the junction at Dunton Green.

The next recorded happening was on 25th June, 1879, when an Agreement was made between the Westerham Valley Railway Co. and the South Eastern Railway Co. 'for the working, use, management and maintenance of the Westerham Valley Railway by the South Eastern Railway Company'. An Act of Parliament received the Royal Assent on 21st July, 1879 (42 and 43 Vict. cap. 153), conferring further powers to the SER authorising it to subscribe to the funds of the WVR Co.

To celebrate the start of work on actually constructing the branch line there was a banquet in the public hall at Westerham on the evening of 1st October, 1879, attended by WVR and SER people. Colonel Charles Madan Warde of Squerryes was in the chair, and Westerham was represented by William Tipping, Dr C.R. Thompson, A.R. Stenning (surveyor), H.D. Brown, C. Sheath, F. Tipping, W. Fox and R. Durtnell; along with the line's Engineer, John Grover, and contractor, Charles Chambers of Westminster Chambers, Victoria Street, London. South Eastern officials included Sir Edward Watkin, E.H. Knatchbull-Hugessen (Deputy Chairman), John Shaw (Secretary) and F. Brady (Engineer).

Charles Chambers had built the Southwold Railway in 1878-9, but Westerham seems to have been his only railway contract in the south-east, and presumably he was chosen by the WVR rather than the SER. His estimate for the cost of construction was £65,000. Watkin, expressing surprise that the branch line would take 20 months to build, said he hoped he would live to see the opening; he had 'connected with the Westerham Valley Railway to keep good faith with the district' and the line 'ought to have been built years ago'. [*Railway Times*, 4th October, 1879, p. 83]

On leaving Dunton Green station the railway was to run west on a fairly straight and level course, with one intermediate station a mile north of the village of Brasted, to a terminus at Westerham, only a short distance north of the High Street. The branch line would be single throughout, there being no passing places.

During the months that followed, while the branch line was being constructed, the WVR Directors made several requests of the SER for loans of money with which to pay the contractor and for land purchases, as well as repaying the Imperial Bank its loan to the promoters at six per cent interest. By April 1881 the South Eastern had advanced no less than £45,000 to the WVR. The SER Directors were informed in January 1880 that the works were being rapidly proceeded with; all the land required had been purchased except for one acre from Mr Tonge, two acres from Lord Stanhope and two acres from Mr W. Spottiswoode.

From January 1880 the WVR Co. kept a General Meeting Minute Book; this has very few entries and there is no record of anything before then. Perhaps the minutes of earlier meetings were written on scraps of paper! On 8th January, 1880, the promoters of the WVR held a special general meeting at the London Bridge offices of the SER to approve the 1879 Agreement and to elect the

Directors of the WVR Co. for 1880. These were: Sir Edward William Watkin, the Rt Hon. Edward Hugessen Knatchbull-Hugessen (Chairman), Charles Robert Thompson, William Tipping and Lt-Col Charles Arthur Madan Warde. Later that year Hugessen was created 2nd Baron Brabourne.

In July 1880 Sir Edward Watkin learned that Charles Chambers intended to sell his shares in the line. The SER Chairman was not at all happy about this as he feared that if an independent body of shareholders outside the SER existed 'there might be difficulty in arranging as to the line hereafter'. The Board promptly gave Watkin a free hand to keep the shares in SER hands by any means he saw fit. He therefore arranged for Messrs Grieveson, Grant & Co. of Royal Exchange Avenue, London, to purchase from Chambers on behalf of Mr Worsley's Trust (of which Watkin was a trustee), 794 fully paid-up shares in the WVR Co. to prevent their coming on to the market. Effectively, Watkin himself had bought the shares.

Watkin and the Deputy Chairman had a tour of inspection of the line on 20th July, 1880. Francis Brady, the SER's Engineer, had received instructions to prepare plans for a junction platform on the up side of Dunton Green station.

In August 1880 the WVR Co. minutes recorded that the contractor was making rapid progress with the construction of the works and of the stations at Brasted and Westerham. Both station buildings were constructed in the 'cheap' style then favoured by the SER, each being timber framed and weatherboarded, resting on a low brick base, the roofs having slates.

At the next meeting of the WVR Co., on 24th February, 1881, the Directors were told that the works, which were nearly completed, had been very much delayed owing to heavy rains during the latter part of 1880. There had been a great snowstorm on 18th January, 1881, which no doubt had also caused difficulties. The Directors approved the eventual conferring of further powers on the SER, these allowing the dissolution of the WVR and transferring the undertaking to the South Eastern.

The Census of 1881 shows that during April and May at least 13 of the labourers employed on the railway were housed in Westerham: there were eight lodging at the Grasshopper Inn, three lodging in a High Street house, one (William Davis) at Charmans Farm Cottage and one (William Lewis, possibly a local man) in Lodge Lane. Walter Steer, driver of a portable engine, boarded in Duncans Yard. At Brasted Albert Lord, a railway engine driver, is thought to have been in Chambers' employ.

The Westerham Valley Railway Company gave its first notice to the Railway Department of the Board of Trade on 27th April, 1881, of its intention to open the line, and on 27th May gave its second notice, sending plans and documents as required by the Board. Major-General Charles Scrope Hutchinson was appointed to inspect the line for the Board, and he performed this duty in June 1881. This is what he reported:

10th June, 1881

I have the honour to report, for the Board of Trade, that I have inspected the Westerham Valley Railway.

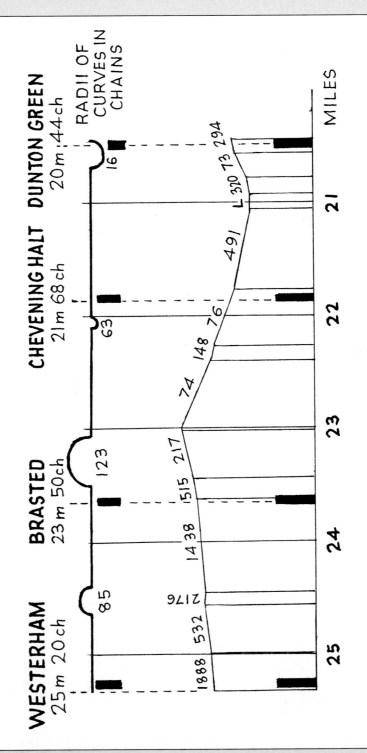

Gradient Profile and Curvature of the Branch

This railway, which is a single line 4¾ miles long, joins the main line of the South Eastern Railway at Dunton Green Station; there is a connection with the up main line only, as it is intended to run only a branch service of trains. The permanent way consists of flat-bottomed steel rails weighing 70 lbs. to the yard, fished at the joints, and secured to cross sleepers by four . . . clips in each sleeper. The sleepers are rectangular 9 ft by 10 in. by 5 in., 2,010 to the mile. The ballast is of shingle and is . . . to . . . a depth of 2 ft below the tops of the rails.

The steepest gradient has an inclination of 1 in 70 and the sharpest curve a radius of 18 chains. Land has been purchased and the overbridges constructed for a double line.

There are several cuttings and banks, the sides of which have been giving much trouble during the past winter. The slips appear to have been now overcome.

There are three bridges under the line, two with iron girders and one with an arched top, and resting on brick abutments. Over the line there are five bridges, entirely of brickwork largest span 14 ft. There are six brick culverts, largest 3 ft wide.

The fencing is of post and wire.

The two stations are Brasted and Westerham, and Dunton Green has been enlarged on the up side. These stations are provided with all necessary accommodation and the signal arrangements have been properly carried out in three new signal cabins, in which they use the necessary block telegraph and speaking instruments.

The line has been well finished, the only requirements I observed were that

1. At Dunton Green a clock visible from the line and safety points for No. 2 Siding were required.
2. The occupation gates should be prevented from opening outwards.

The line is worked by the South Eastern Co. and an undertaking will be required as to the proposed method of working, which should be given by the Westerham Co. and concurred with the S.E. Co.

In consequence of there being no engine turntables this undertaking should provide that all trains should stop at Brasted Station.

Subject to this undertaking and the above requirements I can recommend the Board of Trade not to object to the Westerham Valley Railway being opened for public traffic.

C.S. Hutchinson,
Major-General, R.E.

The exact length of the branch was 4 miles 56 chains and there were rather more than six culverts, as the later bridge number series indicated. Three dots in the above transcription of Hutchinson's report are put in where his handwriting proved indecipherable.

Doubtless the reason the branch had no turntables was that there was still the expectation that it might some day be extended. The SER had almost no tank locomotives, and the Board of Trade disliked the working of lines by engines running tender-first. The likelihood is that the requirement for all trains to call at Brasted was put in as a way of ensuring that there was no chance of trains that were being worked tender-first running too fast.

The Westerham Valley Railway sent the Board of Trade its undertaking on 23rd June, 1881, that the line would be worked by train staff and that all trains would stop at Brasted.

The SER Board decided to have a private opening of the line on 6th July and to give a dinner at Westerham the same evening in honour of all the local promoters of the railway, and then to open the line for public traffic on the 7th.

SOUTH EASTERN RAILWAY

TIMETABLE FOR JULY, AUGUST and SEPTEMBER, 1881

WEEKDAYS

	am	am	am	am	am	pm	pm	pm	pm	pm	A pm	pm
CHARING CROSS dep	5 45	..	8 25	..	11 25	1 40	4 5	5 2	5 55	7 28	8 30	..
CANNON STREET dep	5 57	....	8 35	....	11 35	1 52	4 16	5 13	6 5	7 36	8 40	....
LONDON BRIDGE dep	6 0	..	8 38	..	11 38	1 55	4 19	5 16	6 8	7 39	8 43	..
DUNTON GREEN arr	6 56	....	9 28	....	12 36	2 51	5 7	6 9	7 3	8 26	9 23	....
.. .. dep	7 0	8 10	9 35	11 10	12 40	2 55	5 10	6 15	7 10	8 30	9 25	10 0
Brasted..........	7 7	8 17	9 42	11 17	12 47	3 2	5 17	6 22	7 17	8 37	9 32	10 7
WESTERHAM .. arr	7 10	8 20	9 45	11 20	12 50	3 5	5 20	6 25	7 20	8 40	9 35	10 10

SUNDAYS

		am	am	am		pm		pm	pm	pm	pm	
CHARING CROSS dep	..	7 50	9 0	10 30	..	..	..	2 30	4 10	6 20	..	..
CANNON STREET dep	....	8 0	9 12	10 42	....	....	....	2 40	4 20	6 30	....	....
LONDON BRIDGE dep	..	8 3	9 15	10 45	..	..	..	2 43	4 23	6 33	..	..
DUNTON GREEN arr	....	8 59	10 11	11 39	....	....	....	3 39	5 19	7 25	....	....
.. .. dep	..	9 5	10 15	11 45	..	1 10	..	3 45	5 25	7 30	8 10	..
Brasted..........	....	9 12	10 22	11 52	....	1 17	....	3 52	5 32	7 37	8 17	....
WESTERHAM .. arr	..	9 15	10 25	11 55	..	1 20	..	3 55	5 35	7 40	8 20	..

WEEKDAYS

	am	am	am	am	pm	pm	pm	pm	pm	pm		pm
WESTERHAM .. dep	6 40	7 55	9 0	10 50	12 10	2 15	4 10	5 25	6 50	7 40	..	9 40
Brasted..........	6 43	7 58	9 3	10 53	12 13	2 18	4 13	5 28	6 53	7 43	....	9 43
DUNTON GREEN arr	6 50	8 5	9 10	11 0	12 20	2 25	4 20	5 35	7 0	7 50	..	9 50
..... dep	....	8 8	9 13	11 5	12 25	2 30	4 24	5 40	....	7 55	....	9 54
LONDON BRIDGE arr	..	9 3	10 1	11 57	1 17	3 22	5 14	6 34	..	8 49	..	10 42
CANNON STREET arr	....	9 7	10 5	12 2	1 21	3 26	....	6 38	....	8 53	....	10 46
CHARING CROSS arr	..	9 19	10 17	12 14	1 33	3 38	5 25	6 50	..	9 5	..	10 59

SUNDAYS

		am	am	am	pm		pm		pm	pm	pm	
WESTERHAM .. dep	..	8 45	9 30	11 25	12 50	..	3 25	..	5 5	7 10	7 50	..
Brasted..........	....	8 48	9 33	11 28	12 53	....	3 28	....	5 8	7 13	7 53	....
DUNTON GREEN arr	..	8 55	9 40	11 35	1 0	..	3 35	..	5 15	7 20	8 0	..
..... dep	....	....	9 43	....	1 4	....	....	....	5 49	....	8 7	....
LONDON BRIDGE arr	..	..	10 34	..	1 55	..	..	..	6 33	..	9 1	..
CANNON STREET arr	....	....	10 38	....	1 59	....	....	....	6 37	....	9 5	....
CHARING CROSS arr	..	..	10 51	..	2 12	..	..	..	6 50	....	9 18	..

A - September only.

Westerham prepared to welcome the railway. On the morning of Wednesday 6th July, 1881, the streets and approaches were displaying flags of all colours, and at the entrance to the town was a handsome triumphal arch composed of evergreen and decorated with flags, on one side of which was written in white letters on a red background, 'Success to the Railway' and on the other side, 'Onward' - the motto of the South Eastern Railway. In the High Street, the King's Arms hotel displayed a great quantity of bunting, and the frontage of the Town Hall had festoons and flags in great numbers.

The *Sevenoaks Chronicle* for 8th July, 1881, in reporting the joyous occasion, told its readers that the contract sum for building the branch railway had been £65,000 but, because the soil had proved very treacherous, being wet and marshy, the actual cost amounted to about £70,000. It was still expected that the line would soon be extended to Oxted, although as events proved this was never to happen. Although Oxted was only four miles from Westerham there would have been some severe gradients and heavy engineering works on any line connecting the two places.

The South Eastern Railway was only too well noted for its exorbitant fares, but just for that day the company very generously put on a special service of free trains. The first special left Westerham at noon for Brasted and Dunton Green and back again, conveying Westerham schoolchildren and teachers; then at 1.30 and 3.00 pm further free trains for the use of the general public were run. At 1.30 pm the Tunbridge Wells Parade Band played on Westerham Green.

There could hardly have been greater excitement if Royalty itself were visiting the town, but it was in fact the Chairman of the South Eastern, Sir Edward Watkin himself, who was on that particular day Westerham's most distinguished guest. At 4.10 pm a special train - whose engine was decorated with flags - departed from Charing Cross for Westerham: it conveyed the Chairman; the Deputy Chairman, Lord Brabourne; the General Manager, Myles Fenton; and the Secretary, John Shaw; accompanied by the Directors. On arrival at the tastefully decorated terminus the party alighted and the Parade Band began playing and escorted the procession which formed to the Town Hall, where a grand banquet awaited the honoured guests.

Dr C.R. Thompson said he could remember Westerham in the days when the only communication with London was a daily stage coach which started from the King's Arms at eight in the morning and reached the Borough at eleven, arriving back in Westerham at seven in the evening. Now that the railway was completed the townspeople could look forward to a new era of prosperity. 'I believe the railway will develop industries in the town, and dairy farming, and the extension of the market garden. We shall be able to get coal at a cheaper rate.'

'We now have the privilege of going to London 10 times a day, whereas formerly, by the coach, we could only go there once,' averred Mr Fox. 'To the trade of Westerham this is a great advantage.'

Not only would farmers in the district be able to get their produce conveyed by rail at the same rates as other hitherto more favoured people, and to compete in the London and other markets with their rivals, but the train service would enable 'those gentlemen who were busied in London' every day to live in Westerham and travel daily to town. Westerham would effectively become another suburb of London: a prospect not then regarded with horror but, seemingly, with eagerness. To conclude a momentous day a colourful firework display took place that evening on Westerham Common.

Regular train services began running on the following day, Thursday 7th July, 1881, this being the actual opening day. After the euphoria of the previous day's ceremonial opening, Westerham people soon realised that their new train service was not as marvellous as it might have been. A change at Dunton Green was always necessary in order to get to and from London and, as the South Eastern had no intention of stopping its fast trains at Dunton Green, branch line passengers had to ride in slow trains between the junction and London. Thus, the journey to Charing Cross, which almost always included a diversion into and out of the city terminus of Cannon Street, took about 1½ hours for the 25¼ miles from Westerham to Charing Cross (direct). Still, for a market town of only 2,300 people the service was adequate; and even 20 years later the population had increased by only 600.

The initial timetable showed 11 trains each way between Dunton Green and Westerham on weekdays and eight each way on Sundays. Some of these had no connections with London trains, although they did connect in the opposite direction, to or from Sevenoaks and Tonbridge. On weekdays the first up train, the 6.40 am from Westerham, was useless for London passengers, whose first train was the 7.55 am up which enabled businessmen to be in Cannon Street at 9.07 and Charing Cross at 9.19 - if they were lucky, for SER trains were notoriously unpunctual. The evening service was quite good, passengers for Westerham having a choice of the 4.05, 5.02 and 5.55 pm trains from Charing Cross (Cannon Street 4.16, 5.13 and 6 05 pm). Of these, the first gave the fastest time of the day, 1¼ hours. Late-evening trains were non-existent and passengers had to make sure they caught the 7.28 pm from Charing Cross (Cannon Street 7.36 pm) for the last connecting train from Dunton Green to Westerham, as the 10.00 pm from Dunton Green had no London connection.

All trains were marked as having 1st, 2nd and 'Parliamentary' or 3rd class. The single fare is believed to have been at the rate of 3d. a mile 1st class and 1½d. a mile 3rd, the respective fares between Westerham and Dunton Green being 1s. 3d. and 7½d.: not particularly cheap.

Timetables in those days were revised every month, and intending passengers always had to watch out for these minor alterations or risk missing a train that was now running five minutes earlier than before. From September 1881 an additional evening down train was put on, the 9.25 pm from Dunton Green, which connected with the 8.30 pm from Charing Cross (Cannon Street 8.40 pm). A further improvement, from November 1881, was a late night train on Wednesdays only, leaving Charing Cross at 11.40 pm, with a connection enabling the passenger to be in Westerham at 12.46 am. These extra down trains were not balanced by up ones, which presumably ran as empty stock. The 7.28 pm from Charing Cross now had no branch connection, for the branch train was leaving Dunton Green 25 min. earlier than before and connecting with nothing. The Sunday service was reduced for the winter to five trains each way; irritatingly two of the up trains with London connections were discontinued while three with no connections were kept on.

Chapter Three

The Line Described

The Westerham Valley Railway had its own platform at Dunton Green, on the up side and curving away south-west from the main station, the junction with the up main line being to the north. Dunton Green station (20 miles 44 chains from Charing Cross) was built on a high embankment, the main buildings (of timber) on the up platform with the signal cabin placed north of this platform. By 1909 a new signal cabin on the down side, up end, had replaced the original one. Branch trains could run through from Westerham to Orpington or London without any problem, but down trains for the branch had first to run into the down main platform, then set back over a crossover north of the station before being able to enter the branch platform. Immediately south-west of this platform there were two sidings, by 1909 increased to three, the new one being laid west of the original two.

Access to the station by road from Dunton Green village was very indirect, but foot passengers could use a path from London Road - by the post office and the Duke's Head inn - across the field to the station approach; originally this path crossed the branch on the level but later a subway was built. The branch platform included a run-round loop but originally no headshunt, this being added at the north end about 1917.

When built the WVR was mileposted from the junction and until about 1900 the main line was mileposted from London Bridge; both the main and branch lines then were given new posts taking the mileage from Charing Cross.

Leaving Dunton Green on a curve of 16 chains radius and passing beneath London Road just south of the Duke's Head the branch headed straight for Chevening bridge (where, in 1906, a halt was erected at 21 miles 68 chains). Here was encountered a fairly deep cutting, the only notable engineering work on the line. Chevening and Chevening Park were about a mile to the north-west; Chipstead about half a mile to the south-east.

The next road bridge under which the line passed carried a minor road leading south to Sundridge. Passing through a cutting the line ran beneath the next overbridge, which carried the road to Combe Bank (farm to the north, convent to the south). After a mile of climbing at 1 in 76 or 74 the line then reached the 'summit' at milepost 23, 350 ft above sea level, as it passed through Combe Bank Wood. From here the line fell gently for the rest of its length. At the west end of the wood the line entered a cutting, over which was the last of the five brick-built overbridges (each of which was constructed with an additional arch for a second track if required at some future date), and where there were perennial problems with drainage. The line now entered Brasted station (3 miles 6 chains from Dunton Green, 23 miles 50 chains from Charing Cross).

This station, situated on the south side of the line, had a pleasing well-proportioned timber building and a small signal cabin. There were two goods sidings, of which the southernmost originally had a run-round loop; later the

Dunton Green station in early Southern days, looking north. At the end of the up platform the ramped structure visible was linked by aerial ropeway to the signal cabin to enable the tablet for the branch to be exchanged. A down Hastings train approaches in the distance.   *R.W. Kidner*

The up main platform at Dunton Green, looking south, showing the entrance to the rather gloomy passageway leading to the branch platform.   *Lens of Sutton*

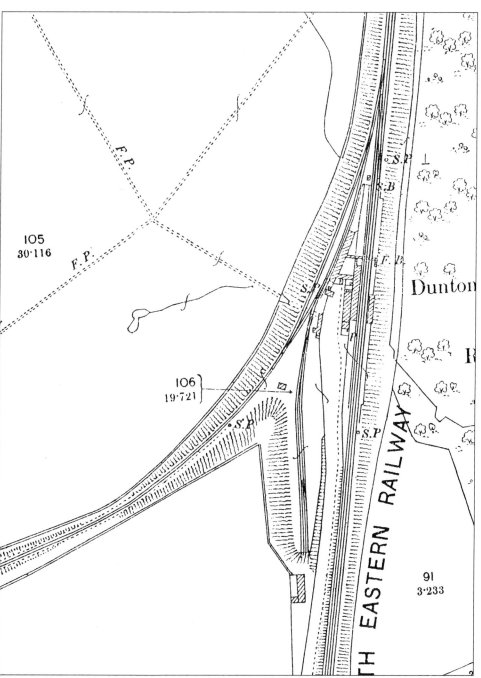

Dunton Green station.   *Reproduced from the 25", 1896 Ordnance Survey Map*

What might be called 'the standard view' of the branch at Dunton Green station: here are class 'H' No. 31512 and Set 482. The picture may be dated to 1959 because the engine was allocated to Tonbridge in that year and the carriages were withdrawn in March 1960.   *Lens of Sutton*

Push-and-pull set No. 723 is propelled from Westerham (dep. 12.23 pm) into Dunton Green by class 'H' No. 31520 on 14th May, 1960.   *James Aston*

Three bicycles left at the top of the steps that led down to Chevening Halt, and the notice of forthcoming closure next to a poster advertising a Shopping Ticket to London (4s. 9d., Wednesday and Thursday only), are almost the only indication of the presence of a railway here in the late summer of 1961. *Lens of Sutton*

A view of Chevening Halt looking towards Westerham, c. 1961. *Lens of Sutton*

Chevening Halt, as rebuilt in concrete and showing recently renewed bridge on 19th April, 1952; view looking east.   *James Aston*

Brasted station seen on 19th April, 1952.   *James Aston*

The station name at Brasted formed in white pebbles, photographed on 5th May, 1934.

L.T. Catchpole

Brasted station.   *Reproduced from the 25″, 1896 Ordnance Survey Map*

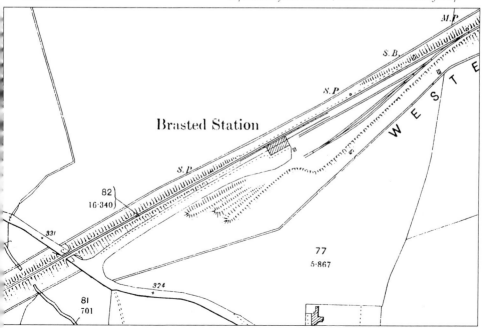

Above: Bridge No. 1441 between Brasted and Westerham, 18th April, 1965. The down distant signal (fixed) is just visible in the background of this view looking north-east. *Author*

Right: Bridge No. 1441 from the south-east on 14th February, 1966, when the track was still intact. The headroom of the bridge was 12 ft 3 in. *Author*

Below: This wrought-iron bridge to the south-west of Brasted station, crossing the lane from the village, was still intact in June 1969 although the track over it had been lifted. *Author*

westernmost points were removed and the loop then became a third siding. When the signalling and signal cabin were removed (probably in the early 1920s) the entry to the sidings was then controlled by a 3-lever ground frame. There was never a goods shed but there were three huts around the yard and by the 1930s a former London, Brighton & South Coast Railway goods van body, still with its 'W' irons, had been placed in the yard as a store. It, and the coal yard, were still in use in 1965, after the station had been closed. Also, by the 1930s, the staff had set out beside the track opposite the platform the station name in whitewashed stones, with a neat border in the same material, set in clean black ash, some 20 feet long; this decorative display was still there in 1963. Combined with the trimmed bushes, fluted cast-iron lampposts and the porter's typical two-wheeled barrow, Brasted could be said to have been a 'model' station in real life. But for passengers it was not very convenient, being not only more than half a mile from the village but well off the road, from which it was reached by a long sloping approach road.

Continuing, the railway crossed over the road that led south-east to Brasted church and village; then over a road leading to Force Green; both these bridges had iron girders resting on brick piers and were built for a single line only with no provision for a second track.

Westerham station (4 miles 56 chains from Dunton Green, 25 miles 20 chains from Charing Cross), which was entered after a straight run of ¾ mile, was quite well equipped although it never looked as if it were intended to function as a terminus. The station building (on the north side of the line), the medium-sized goods shed, the small 13-lever signal cabin and the one-road engine shed were all built of timber with brick bases. There was a large iron water tank supported on six spindly legs and, nearby, a water column for locomotives to replenish their supply.

The goods yard was quite substantial. Originally there was one long siding, connected to the run-round loop by sets of points both west and east of the goods shed, through which the siding passed. A yard crane with a lifting capacity of five tons and a lifting height of 17 ft 6 in. stood on a round plinth a few yards north-east of the goods shed, inside which was another crane which could lift one ton at a height of 12 ft. By 1909 an additional siding to the south of the existing one had been added, the 'Back Siding'.

Right at the end and on the south side of the running road there was a loading dock - a most unusual location, for to use it side-loading vehicles had to stand on the running line, hard against the buffer stops.

By 1896 there was a timber yard (later Horton's) immediately to the south-east of the station and later a granary, with a 'gangplank' connection to the goods yard.

Some years after the opening the station building was given a short extension in matching style at the north-east end, but as the canopy was not extended with it the building now looked curiously 'unbalanced'. In the 1920s the window at the south-west end was taken out and the wall made good; a small room (apparently used for dumping ashes) at this end was at the same time stripped and converted into a through walkway between the forecourt and the platform.

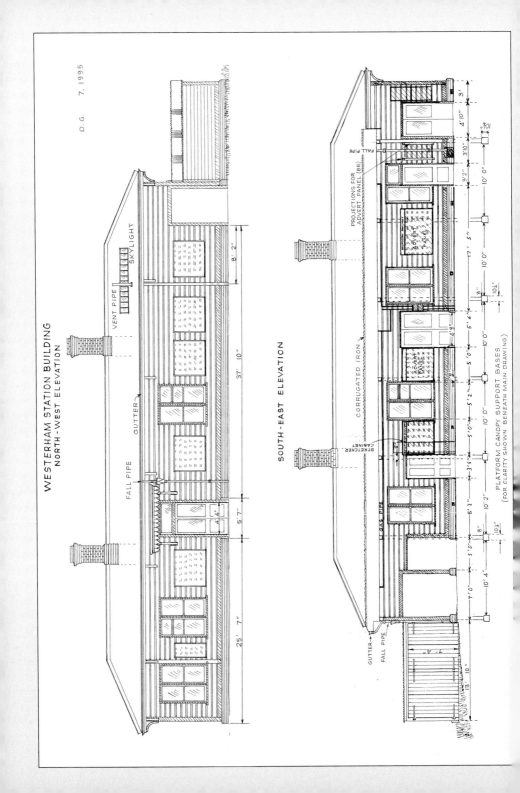

WESTERHAM STATION BUILDING
NORTH-WEST ELEVATION

SOUTH-EAST ELEVATION

D.G. 7.1995

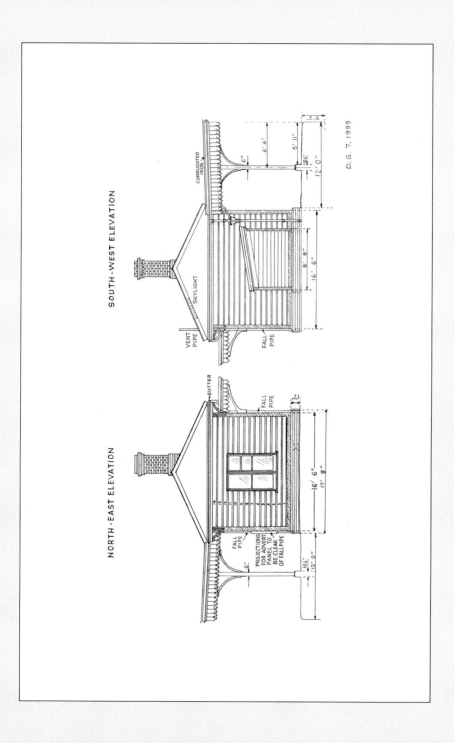

Westerham station.

Reproduced from the 25", 1896 Ordnance Survey Map

Westerham station goods starting signal, the only SE&CR signal and wooden post to survive right until the line's closure. Apparently it had recently been painted when this picture was taken in June 1950.   *Denis Cullum*

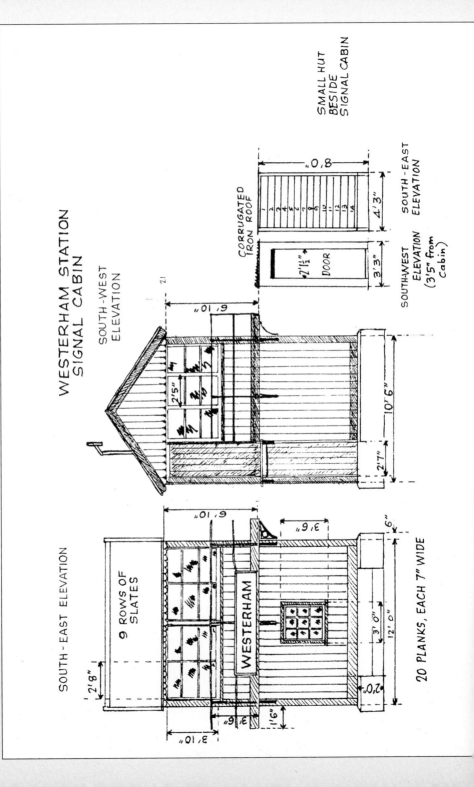

WESTERHAM STATION
SIGNAL CABIN

SOUTH-WEST
ELEVATION

SOUTH-EAST ELEVATION

9 ROWS OF
SLATES

2'8"

WESTERHAM

3'10"

6'10"

3'6"

3'6"

1'6"

3'6"

3'0"

12'0"

2'0"

6"

20 PLANKS, EACH 7" WIDE

6'10"

2'5"

3'10"

10'6"

2'7"

21

SMALL HUT
BESIDE
SIGNAL CABIN

SOUTH-EAST
ELEVATION

8'0"

4'3"

CORRUGATED
IRON ROOF

1 2 3 4 5 6 7 8 9 10 11 12 13 14

DOOR

2'1½"

3'3"

SOUTHWEST
ELEVATION
(3'5" from
cabin)

Westerham station signal cabin, *c.* 1958. Also in this picture are the SR replacement upper-quadrant up starting signal, a 'C' sign indicating a temporary speed restriction, and the signalman's bicycle.   *D. Tutt*

Westerham lamp hut seen on 26th September, 1964.   *D.L. Miller*

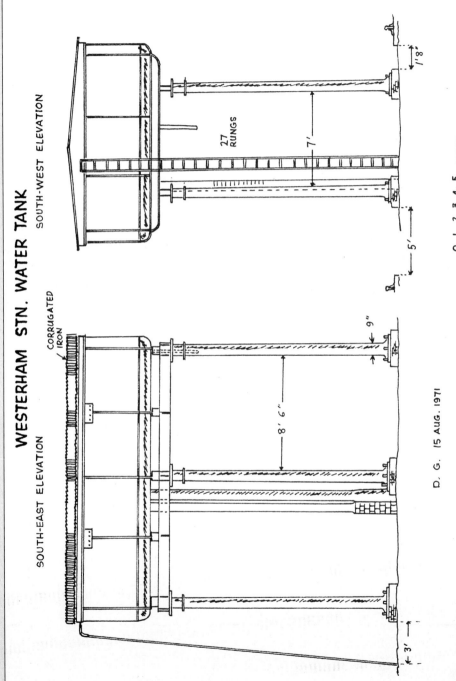

WESTERHAM STN. WATER TANK

SOUTH-EAST ELEVATION

SOUTH-WEST ELEVATION

CORRUGATED IRON

27 RUNGS

1' 8"

7'

5'

9"

8' 6"

3'

SCALE: 0 1 2 3 4 5 FEET

D. G. 15 AUG. 1971

Westerham station had not long to go when this scene of 14th February, 1966, was recorded, and the signal cabin had already vanished. Prominent is the low base of the former engine shed with its curious iron railings.   *Author*

Westerham station water tank from the south, 28th June, 1964, when the WVRA was still active.
                                                                                                    Author

WESTERHAM STATION GOODS SHED

SOUTH-EAST ELEVATION

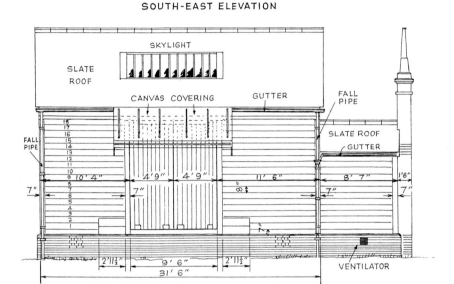

NORTH-WEST ELEVATION

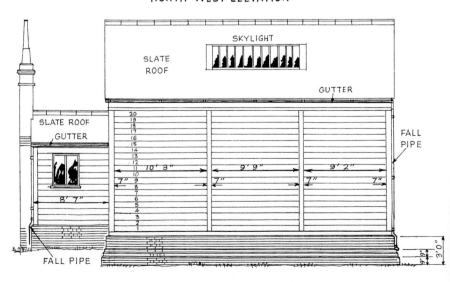

SOUTH-WEST ELEVATION

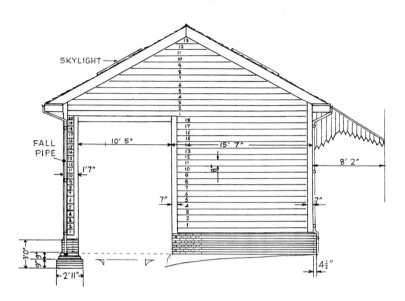

NORTH-EAST ELEVATION

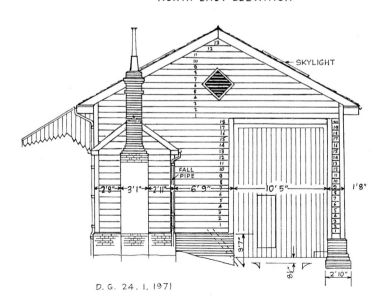

D. G. 24. 1. 1971

Two views of Westerham goods shed; the first in August 1961 in late BR days; the second view on 26th September, 1964, in WVRA days.   *(Both) D.L. Miller*

Above: The interior of the goods shed at Westerham in September 1964 showing the small crane.
Below: The yard crane at Westerham in September 1964. *(Both) D.L. Miller*

The goods shed was a slightly odd structure too. The ground on which it was built dropped slightly from south-east to north-west and to accommodate this the brick base of the shed's north-west elevation was about a foot lower than the bases of the other three sides. All four walls were of shiplap weatherboarding, in contrast to the rebated weatherboarding of the station building.

Perhaps the oddest building of all, however, was the engine shed. Made of timber, on a brick base, it could hold one small locomotive and the roof had a curved cross-section. There was an ash-pit inside the shed. In October 1881 there was a great storm over much of south-east England and although the *Sevenoaks Chronicle* is silent about any damage thus caused to buildings locally it seems that Westerham's little engine shed was damaged to some extent, on the night of 11th October. Some months later the structure was repaired and. given a new roof of normal pitched type. The shed, originally only about 39 ft long, was extended to about 50 ft.

In later years engine workings were altered so that locomotives no longer stabled at Westerham overnight, and about 1925 the shed was closed and subsequently demolished; the ash pit was filled in and totally-superfluous post-and-rail iron fencing was erected on the dwarf walls that remained.

To the north of the Westerham Valley Railway ran the so-called Pilgrim's Way from west to east, and to the south ran the Darent River in the same direction. Only small tributary streams feeding this river needed to be bridged by the railway. Although there were only eight major bridges there were a great many culverts and when bridge number plates were later fixed their numbers ran from 1415 to 1445.

Westerham station from London Road, in about August or September 1961, after the closure notice had gone up. By October the large poster in front of the station building had been replaced by one proclaiming 'Beer - it's lovely!'   *Lens of Sutton*

Chapter Four

South Eastern Railway

On 11th August, 1881, a further Act of Parliament received the Royal Assent (44 and 45 Vict. cap. 195); this provided for the dissolution of the Westerham Valley Railway Co. and transferring the undertaking to the SER.

About the last act of the WVR Co. before its winding-up was to hand over a cheque to the SER for £1,018, which was the credit balance of its account with the National Provincial Bank; this was done on 23rd September, 1881. The SER itself paid various sums to landowners, surveyors and solicitors for additional lands purchased, and there was even a claim of £20 from a Mr Skelton for damage to crops during the building works, and as well as a claim of £7 10s. from a Mr Barrett for damage to his land caused by a landslip on the railway.

A revised undertaking as to the mode of working the branch was sent in to the Board of Trade on 27th February, 1882, by Myles Fenton, the General Manager. In what way it differed from the original undertaking of June 1881 is unknown, as that document was returned to the SER from the BoT. The revised undertaking, however, has survived:

27th February, 1882

Working of Westerham Valley Single Line

The South Eastern Railway Company hereby undertake that the following mode of working the Westerham Valley line will be adopted, viz:

That the line shall be worked by train staff in the mode described in Section II of the Board of Trade amended Regulations for working single lines, combined with the absolute Block Telegraph system.
All trains on this line will stop at Brasted Station.

Witness
John Shaw
Secretary
South Eastern Railway Co.

An advertisement that appeared in the *Sevenoaks Chronicle* for 4th November, 1881, placed by Charles Chambers, the contractor of the Westerham line, gives a good indication of just what equipment was used during the construction. It included a Hunslet 0-6-0 tank engine with 13 in. cylinders, a Manning, Wardle 0-4-0 tank engine with 8 in. cylinders, 200 tons of flat-bottom rails, a large quantity of tip wagons, a 6 hp portable steam engine by Davey, Paxman of Colchester, and various offices and temporary buildings. All these were auctioned at Dunton Green and Brasted on 15th November, 1881.

In September 1881 William Tipping informed the SER that the inhabitants of Brasted were willing to build a road to the station if the company would pay £100 towards the cost of doing so; to this proposal the latter agreed.

Presumably there was only a rough track or path leading to the station from the public road.

A year later the SER entered into an agreement with Samuel Wreford, owner of the Dunton Green Brick and Tile Works, by which the company would build a subway under the branch line, a short way south of the branch platform at Dunton Green. This subway, which was opened in early December 1882, replaced two level crossings: one on the main line just north of the station and one on the branch line some distance west of the station. The new subway, for pedestrians only, connected a footpath to the village on the west side of the station with the approach road between the main line and branch platforms. South of the station was a public road that ran past Wreford's Brick and Tile Works, which was on the east side of the main line.

In May 1882 the SER decided to build an intermediate station at Sundridge and the Engineer was told to prepare a plan and estimate the cost without delay; despite this initial sense of urgency, however, the station was never built. Nor was a proposed house for the station master at Westerham: the Board in October 1883 putting off a decision until the following spring. The land later became railwaymen's allotments. A house for the station master at Brasted was first proposed in October 1882 and similarly put off, but in 1883 this house actually was built, at a cost of about £560 - and, curiously enough, still survived in 1995.

The train service on the branch was arranged to start and finish at Westerham, where the engine was stabled overnight. Tonbridge was the main shed for the district, and possibly motive power was exchanged during the middle of the day at Dunton Green. Only second-rank locomotives and carriages would have been seen on the branch during the 1880s .

The earliest Working Timetable that has come to light is dated June 1883. It shows 13 down trains, plus a late-night Wednesday train from Dunton Green at 12.36 am; 11 up trains, plus one empty and an extra empty on Wednesday evenings. A goods train left Dunton Green at 10.15 am, calling at Brasted 10.30, and arrived at Westerham 10 minutes later. The up goods departed at 8.25 pm, calling at Brasted 8.50, and was due at the junction 10 minutes later. The whole service, passenger and goods, was arranged so that it could have been worked by one engine. There was a gap in the morning passenger service to allow a 'path' for the goods; carriages were left at Westerham between 9.45 and 11.00 am and the branch engine ran light to Dunton Green to work the down goods. In the evening there was no such gap; the 8.05 pm from Dunton Green arrived at Westerham, its engine worked the up goods, then another passenger train left the junction at 9.25 pm. It would thus appear that the 8.25 pm goods from Westerham also conveyed the empty carriages to form the 9.25 pm train.

On Sundays during June 1883 there were six trains each way and no goods service; there was a lengthy gap in the middle of the day and a note stated that 'Brasted and Westerham Signals are closed on Sundays from 11.0 am until 3.10 pm'. (In South Eastern terminology 'Signals' was a signal cabin.)

The 6.40 am up from Westerham still had no London connection; the next train, the 7.55 am, was the first to do so, with a booked arrival at Cannon Street of 9.07 and Charing Cross 9.19. The 8.55 am from Westerham connected into a slow train to Cannon Street, due 10.05. Evening trains were better, with the 4.05 pm from Charing Cross (Cannon Street 4.15), the 4.55 (Cannon Street 5.08) and the 5.55 pm (Cannon Street 6.05) all providing good connections. Of these, the 4.55 pm was the fastest, calling only at London Bridge and Chislehurst for a booked arrival at Dunton Green of 5.52, the Westerham connection being due there at 6.06 pm. There were as yet no through trains, but that improvement was to come later. The last down train with a branch connection left Charing Cross at 8.30 pm (Cannon Street 8.40) except on Wednesdays when the 11.40 pm from Charing Cross gave a connection.

By October 1883 the 6.20 pm from Dunton Green to Westerham had been discontinued, so that there were now 12 down trains (13 on Wednesdays) and 11 up ; on Sundays there were five in each direction, with nothing moving between 11.55 am and 7.10 pm.

Goods traffic at this period included incoming coal and outgoing beer; and in all probability the wagons also conveyed timber, agricultural implements and produce, cattle and flowers from local market gardens. Among the advertisers in *The Westerham Herald* for 1st October, 1883, were some who could well have sent their products by rail. There was the Westerham Brick Yard and Pottery Works, in London Road, making bricks, tiles and ornamental pottery. There was E. Dye & Son, of Market Place, Westerham; this firm made agricultural implements and were furnishers and wholesale ironmongers. W.W. Barton of Brasted was a miller, corn, cake, coal and coke merchant, and his advertisement specifically stated that he had depots at Brasted, Westerham and Sevenoaks stations.

Westerham had two breweries: one, the Swan Brewery at the bottom of Vicarage Hill, closed about 30 years after the railway opened; the other, the Black Eagle Brewery, having been amalgamated with the Swan in July 1897, moved to new premises at the western edge of the town in 1899. This advertised 'weekly deliveries'. Hops were grown in the fields between Brasted and Westerham, and there were nurseries too; boxes of flowers, fruit and vegetables were sent by train to London, for Covent Garden Market.

The new manager of the King's Arms Hotel, T.P. Grayson, advertised himself in October 1883 as an Agent to the South Eastern Railway Company, and owned 'horses and carriages of the best description'; possibly he had the sole right to convey passengers by carriage from the station forecourt.

In July and August 1884 the South Eastern's passenger timetable for the Westerham branch again showed 13 down trains, plus the late-night Wednesday train, and 12 up trains on weekdays. The extra up train ran at 9.10 pm, presumably replacing the 8.25 pm up goods, which may have been retimed to run earlier. In the down direction the 6.20 pm was not restored but instead there was an extra train at 4.18 pm from Dunton Green returning empty to form the 5.10 pm to Westerham.

Fares between Charing Cross, Cannon Street, London Bridge and Westerham were quoted in the timetable book. These were:

	First	Second	Third
Single	5s. 0d.	3s. 6d.	1s. 9d.
Return	7s. 6d.	5s. 6d.	3s. 6d.

Prices were very stable in the latter part of the 19th century, and a surviving 3rd class single ticket issued from London Bridge to Westerham on 13th May, 1898, displays the fare 1s. 9d. - no increase in 14 years!

In 1884, following the opening of the Croydon, Oxted and East Grinstead line on 10th March, Westerham's landowners began thinking again of extending the Westerham branch to Oxted. A public meeting, at which Col Warde presided, was held in Westerham on 15th December, 1884, to consider the possibility of linking the two lines. The proposed railway, which would have cost about £70,000, would have been about 4½ miles long and served the village of Limpsfield, a mile east of Oxted. If built the line would have given Westerham a choice of route to London, in addition to communication with Croydon, Crystal Palace, Brighton and the south coast. William Tipping, JP, of Brasted Park, was one of those still keen on realising the original aims of the 1876 Bill, and at the meeting he proposed a resolution in favour of the project. The owner of Westerham Hall estate said he would provide funds for obtaining a new Bill, and a committee was appointed. Whatever it may have discussed, nothing concrete emerged, and the extension was never built. The South Eastern successfully petitioned against the Westerham & Oxted Railway in 1885.

In the 1880s Cheap Day tickets were issued every Wednesday from both Westerham and Sevenoaks to London, available by certain trains. *Kelly's Directory* to Kent for 1891 shows that the station master at Westerham was one Charles William Wood; he is known to have held that position between 1890 and 1895. The railway station was linked with the King's Arms by an omnibus which met all the incoming trains. Additionally, two omnibuses daily each way ran between Westerham and Oxted. Surprisingly, John Cumplen's carriers cart still plied twice weekly between Westerham and the Spur Inn, Borough: outward on Mondays and Thursdays, returning on Tuesdays and Fridays.

The Census for the same year indicated that several railwaymen were living at both Westerham and Brasted, for even small stations such as those required fairly large staffs. In Brasted dwelt the station master, John Shoobridge (the station house being of sufficient size to house him, his wife and six children!); a signalman, Thomas Harvey (in Station Road); Charles Cramp, another signalman, in Church Lane; Richard Phillips, a platelayer; and Fred Richardson, a clerk aged only sixteen. Many of these were local men, although initially staff taken on had to be drafted in from outside the area. In Westerham there was an engine driver aged 38, Isaac Cranford, and a 22-year-old fireman who, along with guard Ives, lived in Railway Cottages. Other railwaymen in Westerham included Joseph Fields, a clerk; Robert Howett, a porter ; John Read, an engine cleaner aged 61; and, most remarkably, a 77-year-old platelayer named Joseph Bye. Another guard resident in the town was John Rose, aged 60. None of these men had been born locally. Westerham's signalman has not been traced; perhaps he lived outside the town.

In the 1890s the motive power for the branch was the '118' (later 'E') class 2-4-0 built between 1860 and 1875 during the reign of James I'Anson Cudworth, locomotive superintendent from 1845 to 1876. All had been reboilered, and D.L. Bradley records that Nos. 17, 145, 191, 244, 247 and 252 were based at Tonbridge Shed in 1895 to work the Westerham branch, among others. All were withdrawn between 1901 and 1905. As rebuilt with Stirling boilers, steam-reverse gear and right-hand drive, they were reclassified 'E1'. N. Wakeman, in *The South Eastern & Chatham Railway Locomotive List* (1953) noted that Nos. 68 and 252 were in addition fitted with tender weatherboards. Either No. 17 or No. 252 was the engine usually seen at Westerham sub-shed in late 1897, and No. 68 was transferred to Tonbridge in about 1902.

Gibson Thompson, in his guide book to Westerham and its surrounds, entitled *Wolfe-land* and published about 1897, had this to say about the railway and other methods of transport:

> Leaving the metropolis from Charing Cross, Cannon Street or London Bridge, one journeys to this uncut gem of Nature by the main line of the South Eastern Railway as far as Dunton Green, and thence a 'change' is made to the little toy train of the Westerham Valley Railway, which has a station at Brasted and its terminus at Westerham, and which looks forward to extending itself, some day, to Limpsfield and Oxted.

Thompson may have thought that extension was inevitable, but by that time any such hopes were pretty well buried. The SER was firmly against projecting the line beyond Westerham, and always had been.

To Thompson an immediate attraction just across the road from Westerham station was the Crown Hotel: 'A new building, but withal most comfortable of quarters, as the author from personal experience here testifies.'

Postal arrangements were good. For an additional fee of 2*d.* one could dispatch a letter or parcel by any passenger train from Westerham station.

Thompson gives the times of the omnibuses on the Oxted-Westerham service. Departures from Oxted station were at 7.30 am, 1.00 and 7.00 pm; and from Westerham to Oxted at 8.15 am and 4.30 pm. On Sundays the horse 'bus left Oxted at 11.15 am and 8.30 pm, returning from Westerham at 7.30 pm. This curiously imbalanced timetable cannot be explained.

In noting that Cumplen's carrier's cart was still plodding its way twice weekly between Westerham and London, Thompson also considered the coach services of years past. There was one from the White Hart, Westerham, via Westerham Hill to the Bull & Mouth, Fleet Street, doing the double journey in a day. A later coach service via Botley Hill to Croydon and London ran for a year but ceased in 1848 after losing its proprietor £400. The opening of the railway had killed off the Westerham to Sevenoaks bus; this had run twice daily, with departures from Westerham at 8.00 am and 5.00 pm. There had also been an omnibus that left Westerham at 7.15 am for Caterham station between 1874 and 1878.

Receiving incoming coal and coke at Westerham station in the 1890s was B. Horton, the local merchant, who was still advertising 'cheap coal' in 1906. The railway dealt with the beer traffic in connection with the Black Eagle Brewery, which advertised weekly delivery of its product. Although this brewery was destined to survive the railway, it closed in the 1980s and the once-famed Westerham Ales are no more.

The residents of Brasted and the surrounding area were deeply saddened by the death, in January 1897, of the popular Squire William Tipping. He was still remembered as late as 1961 when, in an article in *The Times* for 11th August that year, he was described as 'tall, with a bald head and grey curls, whiskers and a Newgate frill, walking about wearing a square-topped hard felt hat'. In 1885 he had again been elected MP for Stockport.

Westerham station in 1905, before the main building had been extended at the north-east end. A class 'Q' 0-4-4 tank locomotive is on the branch train in the platform, another engine is in the locomotive shed and yet another outside the goods shed. Behind the timber bolsters can just be seen what is almost certainly the 'Peebles' steam railcar, which was tried out on the branch.

E. Pouteau

Westerham station from London Road in SE&CR days, but after the main building had been extended at the north-east end. *E. Ashby Series*

Chapter Five

South Eastern & Chatham Railway

With the coming together of the South Eastern and its old rival the London, Chatham & Dover (LC&D) under a Managing Committee in 1899 travelling conditions for the passengers began to improve. Although separate diréctorates were retained, operationally the railways were worked as though they were one concern. There were new locomotives, a new livery of Brunswick green, elaborately lined out, new carriages and a more efficient method of working the trains.

To replace the elderly Cudworth engines the Westerham branch now received some examples of James Stirling's class 'Q' 0-4-4 tank locomotives, first introduced in 1881 for suburban work. Some of these very useful little engines were allocated to Tonbridge, and from 1899 to the early part of 1906 the regular branch locomotive of this class was No. 366, which used the Westerham sub-shed. Between 1893 and 1898 Westerham Shed was often host to a class 'O' 0-6-0 goods locomotive, No. 296, which was fitted with a tender weatherboard. In the late 1890s class 'Q' No. 73 also put in an appearance on the branch train, a lengthy caravan comprising a four-compartment Second, three three-compartment Firsts, two Thirds and a brake van, all four-wheeled. These carriages, which in all probability dated from the 1860s, were soon to be replaced by six-wheeled stock built in the 1880s and 1890s, a typical early-20th century train comprising a SER elliptical-roofed six-compartment Third, a LC&D five-compartment Third, a LC&D four-compartment First and a LC&D three-compartment Second Brake. The former London, Chatham & Dover Railway carriages were transferred to the South Eastern just as soon as they had been converted from air- to vacuum-braking and given electric lighting.

One of the biggest improvements on the branch, however, was the introduction of a through train to London (Cannon Street) for businessmen. The precise date that it started is uncertain but it was running by November 1900. Departure time from Westerham was at 8.40 am and an additional portion was attached at Chislehurst. The branch service comprised 13 up and 14 down trains on weekdays, plus an extra late train at 12.47 am from Dunton Green on Wednesday nights/Thursday mornings. The daily goods, at 9.50 am from Dunton Green and 8.20 pm from Westerham, was worked probably by the branch engine, between passenger trips.

In July 1902 the goods trains were retimed: the down train left Dunton Green at 7.55 am, having arrived on the 5.25 am from Bricklayers Arms (this train did not work on Mondays), and the up train left Westerham at 10.45 pm for Dunton Green and Bricklayers Arms - which was the SER's main goods depot in London, just off the Old Kent Road near Bermondsey. Leaving Westerham, the 8.40 am passenger train was formed of both the through carriages to London and the branch train, this being detached at Dunton Green. Sunday service comprised six passenger trains each way.

By February 1904 there were 14 trains each way, Mondays to Fridays; an extra late train on Wednesdays; 13 trains each way on Saturdays and seven on

Sundays. The 7.45 am Dunton Green to Westerham - which formed the 8.40 am up - used stock that had been worked down the main line empty from Rotherhithe Road carriage depot on Mondays or Chislehurst on other days.

Special instructions governed the working of the branch goods trains as shown in the February 1904 Working Timetable:

5.25 am Bricklayers Arms to Westerham
Conveys all Trucks for Dunton Green and Westerham Branch. Brasted Trucks to be taken on to Westerham to be worked back by Special Trip at a convenient time. This Train must not be allowed to delay the Westerham Branch Passenger Working, and if necessary Dunton Green to arrange for the Goods to be kept at Knockholt until prepared to deal with the Train. When unable to follow 7.45 am Westerham Branch Train closely from Dunton Green, the Goods to be kept back to follow the 9.17 am Down Branch Train. When this Train cannot clear Dunton Green Trucks out and it is necessary to run a second trip to that station for them, Westerham to arrange for such Special Trip to run at a suitable time between Passenger Trains using the Branch Engine and Guard for the Service.

11.0 pm Westerham to Bricklayers Arms
The Westerham Branch Engine to be attached to this Train as far as Dunton Green and afterwards return light to Westerham with the Train Staff except on Wednesdays and Saturdays. On Saturday nights the 11. 0 pm Westerham to Bricklayers Arms Goods to carry the Train Staff to Dunton Green, leaving it there for collection by the 4.30 am Sunday Goods from Bricklayers Arms to Westerham.
Beer Traffic from Westerham for the Down Main Line to be attached to the front part of the train.

Several train guards were attached to Westerham during 1904. For working goods and ballast trains: head guard Watts and under guard Pierce. For working passenger trains: Hutchings, Gurr and Shapcott. Gurr was to put in many years of railway service, along with four other Gurrs who were railwaymen until the 1940s. Alfred Gurr, a royal train guard, died in 1913.

The Managing Committee decided in November 1902 to purchase two houses in Westerham for £500 as accommodation for railway staff, including the station master; where they had been living until then is not clear.

At the General Purposes Sub-committee meeting of the (SE&CR) on 27th October, 1903, the General Manager (Vincent Hill) reported that there was considerable delay and much unnecessary light-engine running on the Westerham line caused by the necessity of getting the train staff to one end of the branch or the other. There was only one train staff on the line and with an 'unbalanced' train service it could often happen that the train staff was at the wrong end of the line when required for the next train; hence the light-engine running. With the new electric train staff system, several staffs were in the apparatus but before one of them could be taken out another had first to be replaced in the apparatus at the other end of the line. The decision was taken to re-equip the Westerham line with the electric staff system at a cost of £57 15s., and by April 1904 it had been installed.

Consequently, from May 1904 the working of the branch engine to Dunton Green attached to the 11.00 pm Westerham to Bricklayers Arms and returning light to Westerham with the train staff was discontinued.

Further minor changes in the working of the through passenger trains occurred in July 1904. Stock for the 7.45 am Dunton Green to Westerham and 8.40 am thence to Cannon Street (due 9.34 am) came empty from Tonbridge on Mondays and from Rotherhithe Road on other days. Formation was one First, one Second, one Third and one brake van. Additional carriages, berthed at Westerham, were formed in the 8.40 am up; these returned as part of the 11.56 pm (not Saturdays) or 5.00 pm (Saturdays) from Charing Cross, being detached at Dunton Green and due to arrive at Westerham at 6.07 pm. An extra Third was run in the 4.56 pm down on Tuesdays and the 8.40 am up on Wednesdays.

The branch service on weekdays comprised 13 trains each way, the first one still being the 6.40 am Westerham to Dunton Green and the last, except on Wednesdays, the 10.56 pm Dunton Green to Westerham. On Wednesday nights/Thursday mornings an empty train ran from Westerham to form the 12.45 am Dunton Green to Westerham, after which engine and carriages were put away for the night.

From October 1904 there was another change in the working of the 7.45 am Dunton Green to Westerham and 8.40 am Westerham to Cannon Street: the stock - four Firsts, two Seconds, four Thirds and a brake van - ran empty from Orpington to Dunton Green in the morning and finished the day with the 9.14 pm Charing Cross to Orpington.

In common with other railways in the mid-1900s the SE&CR became very interested in steam railcars, seeing them as a way of beating the electric tramways at their own game. In 1905 a geared steam car built by Ganz of Budapest and reassembled by the Brush Electrical Engineering Co. of Loughborough was introduced into Britain by the Peebles Steam Car Co. of 25 Victoria Street, London, and tried out on the Midland Railway on 2nd June; in the party of railway officers watching the trials was E.C. Cox, of the SE&CR. The 'Peebles' was also given a trial on the Westerham branch but was not purchased. In fact the SE&CR had already ordered from Kitson of Leeds two steam railmotors of the 'detachable' type, in which the engine was articulated to the carriage.

The 'Peebles' car was completely self-contained, with a vertical water-tube boiler in an engine compartment at one end of the vehicle. The engine did not drive the wheels directly but was connected with the driving axle through clutches and gears. This high-speed, two-cylinder, compound engine was hung from the underframe of the car rather like an electric motor and, being separate from the boiler, it could be removed quite easily for maintenance without interfering with the truck and wheels. [*Cassier's Magazine*, September 1905, p. 390.] The car had a bogie at the engine end (with drive on to one axle) and a single axle at the other end.

Although these Ganz railcars operated successfully in Hungary, none of the British railways was interested, and a 60 ft car with two boilers, and seats for 64 passengers, that was being built by the Brush Electrical Engineering Co. during 1905 was not purchased.

Meanwhile on the branch there were more changes in the stock working from September 1905 when a new through train to London was introduced, the 9.42 am from Westerham. Formed of two Firsts, one Second, three Thirds and two

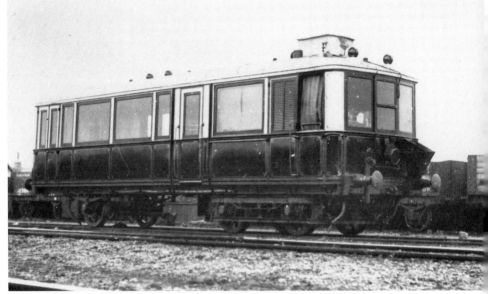

'Peebles' steam railcar, built to the design of Ganz of Budapest with two-cylinder compound engine and geared drive. There was a bogie at one end of the car and two wheels at the other.
R.C. Riley Collection

Steam motor car No. 3 at Westerham during the summer of 1906, with station staff, driver and (probably) guard Gurr posing. The array of posters almost obscuring the station building included 'Country Rambles', 'Red Star Line, Dover-New York' and 'Mr R.K. Griffiths - Freehold Estate'. *A.H. Homewood, Burgess Hill*

brake vans, the empties worked from Bromley North to Dunton Green each morning to form the 9.16 am to Westerham and 9.42 am to London Bridge. A note in the Working Timetable stated that the branch engine and train were to be sent down empty or with the Goods if required at 9.55 am. From October 1905 the through train was formed from empty stock from Orpington and the load reduced to two Firsts, one Second, one six-compartment Third and a brake van. Stock for the 8.40 am up came on to the branch as the 5.10 am from Cannon Street, 6.25 am from Dunton Green, and worked all the branch services until the 8.40 am. The formation was three Firsts, one Second, one six-compartment Third and a brake van. The Westerham-based portion of the 8.40 am (one First, one Second, one Third Brake) returned from Charing Cross in the 4.56 pm except on Saturdays; on Monday mornings this stock came down attached to the 5.10 am from Cannon Street and 6.25 am Dunton Green to Westerham.

Owing to the collapse, on 5th December, 1905, of the Charing Cross station roof and the temporary closure of both that station and Waterloo (SE&CR) main line trains had to be diverted to Cannon Street and elsewhere. To ease the difficulties the 9.42 am from Westerham terminated at Dunton Green, and was restored as a through train on 19th March, 1906, when Charing Cross and Waterloo were reopened.

The two original steam railmotors of 1905 having proved successful on the Sheppey Light Railway and the Chatham Central branch, the SE&CR ordered six more from the same makers: Kitson of Leeds, who made the locomotive portions, and Metropolitan Amalgamated Railway Carriage & Wagon Co., who constructed the carriage portions. They were delivered in March and April 1906. Nos. 3 and 7 were allocated to Orpington and Tonbridge for working the Westerham branch and the Otford to Sevenoaks shuttle.

Each car had a body 48 ft 4 in. long, divided into three portions: a saloon 19 ft 10% in. long for non-smoking passengers, a saloon 14 ft 10% in. long for smokers, and a compartment for luggage, guard and driver, 6 ft 8 in. long. There were two entry vestibules, with inward-opening doors: one at the locomotive end of the car, the other between the smoking saloon and the luggage compartment. Sliding doors gave communication between passengers' and guard's compartments. The interior of the saloon - which contained 56 seats, all third class - was finished in teak. The railmotors were each capable of hauling a trailer coach weighing 16 tons and with such a load able to reach a speed of 30 miles per hour.

On Monday 9th April, 1906, according to The *Westerham Herald* (14th April, 1906), the new railmotor began running on the Westerham Valley line 'and so far, we believe, the experiment has proved a success'. The newspaper also noted: 'There is a trailer for first and second class passengers, the car itself being all one class - third', from which one infers that all trains ran with a trailer attached (usually an LCDR 6-wheeled Brake Composite) and that the steamcar had to run round the trailer at each end of the run. First class season ticket holders would certainly have complained to the General Manager if they had been deprived of the accommodation for which they had paid.

Railmotor No. 3 was more-or-less permanently allocated to Westerham and worked almost all the branch weekday services, beginning with the 10.24 am

SOUTH EASTERN AND CHATHAM RAILWAY

TIMETABLE FOR MAY and JUNE, 1906

WEEK DAYS

DOWN	T	A	Goods NM	T	C	C	C	C SO	C NS	C SO	C SO	C NS
	am	am	am	am	am	pm	pm	pm	pm	pm	pm	pm
Dunton Green dep	6 25	7 45	8 0	9 17	10 48	12 47	2 40	3 23	3 55	3 58	4 55	5 5
Brasted ... dep	6 32	7 53	....	9 24	10 59	12 58	2 51	3 34	4 6	4 9	5 6	5 16
Westerham .. arr	6 36	7 58	8 15	9 27	11 4	1 3	2 56	3 39	4 11	4 14	5 11	5 21

DOWN	C TP NS	C SO	C	C	C	C	C WO mid	T SO mid
	pm	pm	pm	pm	pm	pm	mid	mid
Dunton Green dep	5 55	6 6	7 14	8 4	9 15	10 50	12 46	12 46
Brasted ... dep	6 6	6 17	7 25	8 15	9 26	11 1	12 57	12 54
Westerham .. arr	6 11	6 22	7 30	8 20	9 38	11 6	1 2	12 59

SUNDAYS

DOWN	Goods		E	D					D	E		C
	am	am	am	am	pm	pm	pm	pm	pm	pm	pm	pm
Dunton Green dep	6 0	9 8	10 7	10 12	12 14	4 20	5 24	7 22	7 57	8 5	8 45	10 30
Brasted ... dep	....	9 15	10 14	10 22	12 24	4 30	5 34	7 29	8 7	8 15	8 55	10 41
Westerham .. arr	6 15	9 18	10 17	10 25	12 27	4 33	5 37	7 32	8 10	8 18	8 58	10 46

WEEK DAYS

UP	A	T	T	C	C	C	C SO	C NS	C SO	C SO	C NS	C
	am	am	am	am	pm	pm	pm	pm	pm	pm	pm	pm
Westerham .. dep	7 25	8 40	9 42	10 24	12 15	1 52	3 3	3 28	3†42	4 34	4 43	5 33
Brasted .... dep	7 28	8 43	9 45	10 30	12 21	1 58	3 9	3 34	....	4 40	4 49	5 39
Dunton Green arr	7 36	8 50	9 53	10 38	12 29	2 6	3 17	3 42	3†55	4 48	4 57	5 47

UP	C NS	C SO	C	C	C	B Goods	C SO	C WO mid
	pm	pm	pm	pm	pm	pm	pm	mid
Westerham .. dep	6 18	6 25	7 37	8 53	10 32	11 10	11 15	12†25
Brasted .... dep	6 24	6 31	7 43	8 59	10 38	11z25	11 21	....
Dunton Green arr	6 32	6 39	7 50	9 7	10 46	11 30	11 29	12†38

SUNDAYS

UP								D	E		T
	am	am	am		pm	pm	pm	pm	pm	pm	pm
Westerham .. dep	8 45	9 25	11 53	..	3 50	5 4	6 59	7 40	7 45	8 25	9 5
Brasted .... dep	8 48	9 28	11 56	....	3 53	5 7	7 2	7 43	7 48	8 28	9 8
Dunton Green arr	8 58	9 35	12 6	..	4 2	5 17	7 12	7 50	7 55	8 38	9 15

A—Worked by Engine of 5.10 am from Cannon Street. B—Goods to Bricklayers Arms. On Saturdays will leave Westerham at 11.30 pm. C—Worked by Rail Car and Brake Compo. D—May only. E—June only. T—Through Train. TP—Through Portion. NM—Not Mondays. NS—Not Saturdays. WO—Wednesdays only. SO—Saturdays only. z—Arrive 11.15 pm. †—Empty Train.

All Local Trains run during daylight will call at Chevening Halt when required, except the 6.25, 7.45 and 9.17 am from Dunton Green and the 7.25, 8.40 and 9.42 am from Westerham.

Westerham to Dunton Green and finishing with the 10.50 pm Dunton Green to Westerham. There were 10 return trips Mondays to Fridays, plus a late Wednesday night/Thursday morning journey at 12.46 am from Dunton Green (an empty car running from Westerham to work this). On Saturdays there were 11 down workings and 11 up, plus one empty up in the afternoon; the 11.15 pm (Saturdays) Westerham to Dunton Green continued as empty stock to Orpington, where the car was serviced and the boiler washed-out each Sunday. At 10.10 pm on Sundays the motor left Orpington as a through passenger train to Westerham (due 10.46 pm) for a further week's work on the branch. All other Sunday trains were worked by an ordinary train which had left Orpington at 12.15 am to form the last down train on Saturday nights/Sunday mornings, the 12.46 am Dunton Green to Westerham, and which returned to Orpington on the last up train, the 9.05 pm from Westerham. The car was allowed to work with a Brake Composite if necessary, and the working timetable also noted: 'The Additional Load conveyed by this Vehicle *must not* exceed 2 Ordinary Six-Wheeled Vehicles or 1 Tri-Composite Bogie, or 3 Horse Boxes'.

Trains not worked by the railmotors were: 5.10 am Cannon Street to Westerham, 7.25 am Westerham to Dunton Green and 7.45 am return, 8.38 am Westerham to Cannon Street (three Firsts, one Second, one six-compartment Third, one brake van - plus Brake Composite No. 2063 on the 8.38 am up); and 8.12 am (empty) Cannon Street to Dunton Green, 9.17 am Dunton Green to Westerham, 9.42 am Westerham to Cannon Street (Third Brake, 6-wheel Composite, six-compartment Third, Second, First and brake van). In addition the 5.55 pm (not Saturdays) railmotor from Dunton Green conveyed the through Brake Composite, No. 2063, which had been detached from the 4.56 pm from Charing Cross to Tunbridge Wells.

In connection with the railmotors a new unstaffed halt was opened at Chevening bridge on 16th April, 1906, at a cost - including the nameboard, steps, gates and lamps - of £50. This simple timber platform with a small shelter was situated on the south side of the line, just west of the bridge that carried the road linking the villages of Chipstead and Chevening. Although Chipstead was nearer, its name could not be used for the new Halt as there was already a station named Chipstead on the Tadworth branch.

Until October 1906 Chevening Halt was a request stop, served only by the railmotors and even then only in daylight. Drivers were urged to keep a good lookout for intending passengers and anyone wishing to alight there had to tell the guard. Passengers had to buy their tickets from the guard and there were no through bookings beyond Dunton Green; the guard also was expected to collect tickets from passengers alighting at Chevening Halt. From October 1906 all trains, except the 6.25 am down, called. The Halt was not too well placed but doubtless was intended to serve a fairly large catchment area. In general, Halts stimulated an increase in passenger traffic at minimal cost to the railway, and the *Westerham Herald* believed that another Halt would be opened at some later date at Combe Bank (between Chevening and Brasted) to serve the large estate of that name, rumours having been circulated that it was about to be purchased by a syndicate who intended to convert the mansion into a private hotel and the grounds into a golf course. However, this did not occur and no Halt was ever opened at Combe Bank.

The goods service now included the 5.25 am Bricklayers Arms to Westerham (not Mondays), in which trucks for Brasted were taken on to Westerham, later being worked back by a special trip when convenient; when unable to follow closely the 7.45 am passenger train from Dunton Green the goods was kept back to follow the 9.17 am. Return working of the goods train was at 11.30 pm, calling at Brasted and Dunton Green and continuing to Bricklayers Arms. On Sunday mornings the Westerham goods train left Bricklayers Arms at 4.30 am.

The steam railcars had some drawbacks. One was that they were slow; the journey time on the branch was increased from 10 minutes to 16 minutes down and 14 minutes up, whereas the ordinary trains, even with one extra stop, were booked to take only 11 or 12 minutes either way. Another was that they rode unsteadily, especially when the brake-end was leading, and that first class passengers were deprived of a service unless the Brake Composite was added. Regular passengers did not like the car, presumably because of its bad riding qualities and slowness, and many letters of complaint about it were written to the railway. The car was, after a while, restricted to 25 mph when hauling a trailer.

Whatever the reason - overcrowding or unreliability - No. 3 was withdrawn from the Westerham branch after traffic on 28th February, 1907, and from 1st March an ordinary train and engine took over, the formation being Brake Second, First and Brake Third, all six-wheeled.

Brake Composite No. 2063, Westerham's 'through coach', was a unique vehicle. Built in 1884 with two 1st- and two 2nd-class compartments, it was electro-plated and unpainted, giving it a ghostly look at night time. It was fitted as a slip coach. However, from May 1907 it lost its association with the Westerham Valley line, being transferred to other workings, and was replaced on the 8.38 am Westerham to Cannon Street and 4.56 pm from Charing Cross by six-wheeled Composite No. 2240, which remained on these workings for at least three years except when withdrawn for maintenance. This carriage had been built in 1889 as a Second, altered to Composite and given electric lighting in 1897, but in 1909 had its two lavatory compartments taken out.

Passengers using the footbridge at Dunton Green had been complaining about their lack of protection from the north-easterly gales at this somewhat exposed station, for although the timber bridge had a corrugated-iron roof it was open sided. In 1907 the entire bridge was replaced by one transferred from Grove Park station and completely covered in at a total cost of £375. Around the same time a new house was built for the station master at Dunton Green in replacement of one described as 'very old'.

Branch line services for summer 1909 included 15 trains each way, Mondays to Fridays plus two extra on Wednesdays. On Saturdays there were 18 down and 16 up trains plus two empty up workings. Through trains to London left Westerham at 8.37 and 9.44 am. The 8.37 am to Cannon Street was formed: Train No. 81, plus bogie First and a brake van (which had come down on the 5.10 am Cannon Street to Dunton Green); and a Brake Third, First and Composite No. 2240. An eight-coach train of close-coupled four-wheelers left Orpington empty for Dunton Green to work the 9.17 am to Westerham and 9.44 am up to Cannon Street.

There were goods trains at 4.00 am from Bricklayers Arms to Westerham except on Mondays, and from Westerham back to Bricklayers Arms at 9.45 pm. The 4.00 am conveyed Brasted wagons to Westerham and worked them as a separate trip to Brasted at 8.52 am, returning at 9.10 am. The train engine of the 9.45 pm from Westerham ran from Dunton Green to Sevenoaks to turn, conveying beer traffic from Westerham, and returned to Dunton Green to work the goods to London at 11.43 pm.

D.L. Bradley states that the London trains were worked by Orpington Shed about this time and that Tonbridge Shed provided two class 'Q' 0-4-4 tank locomotives for the branch service, changing over at 3.30 pm. This suggests that Westerham engine shed was no longer in use for overnight stabling of locomotives. It is almost certainly not true, as sometimes stated, that the new class 'P' 0-6-0 tank engines, fitted with mechanical gear for working auto-trains, worked on the branch in 1909, as the first two examples of this class, Nos. 753 and 754, introduced in February 1909, were allotted to the Otford - Sevenoaks and Ash - Aldershot services, according to the Locomotive & Carriage & Wagon Sub-Committee Minutes. Possibly one of these tiny locomotives was tried out on the Westerham Valley some time during 1909, but it appears to be 1913 before any of the class worked regularly on this line. Nos. 325 and 753 are stated to have worked in July 1914. Fitted with a modified type of auto-train gear No. 323 ran in the Sevenoaks area, usually on the Otford push-and-pull service with a LC&D three-coach set of six-wheelers, and may well have taken its turn on the Westerham service. In September 1914 LC&DR class 'R' 0-4-4 tank locomotive No. 675, motor-fitted using compressed air from the Westinghouse pump instead of the mechanical rod system used on the class 'P', underwent brief trials on the Port Victoria, Hawkhurst and Westerham branches. It is stated that this locomotive worked in the centre of the train, which was composed of two three-coach sets of six-wheeled carriages.

Since the trains formed with through carriages had been calling at Chevening Halt, which was a short platform, the inevitable had happened and passengers had been riding in that part of the train projecting beyond the platform when it was brought to a stand at the Halt. To avoid the time-wasting business of 'drawing-up' the staff were instructed to tell any Chevening passengers in the 8.37 am Westerham to Cannon Street to ride in the front portion only, and any for Chevening in the 9.17 am Dunton Green to Westerham and 9.44 am Westerham to Cannon Street to travel in the front two coaches only. In the 8.37 am the guard had to ride in the rear brake of the front portion as far as Dunton Green, where he then changed to the rear van of the train. Formation of the 8.37 am in summer 1910 was van, Train No. 88 (Slip Bogie Composite and Bogie Tri-Composite), Bogie First, Train No. 81. Except on Saturdays Train No. 88 ran in the 4.55 pm Charing Cross to Tonbridge as far as Dunton Green, where it was attached to the 5.58 pm branch train to Westerham (due 6.09 pm).

From October 1910 the fortunate passengers on the 9.44 am Westerham to Cannon Street were provided with the very latest coaching stock, in the shape of a four-coach bogie set (Nos. 104, 105, 106 and 107 in rotation). These were steam-heated (still something of a rarity). The set for the 9.44 am worked up empty from Tonbridge to Dunton Green; incidentally, the 4.55 pm from

Charing Cross to Tonbridge had one of these four-sets also. The 9.44 am through train was, however, discontinued about 1914 although the earlier train continued to run for many more years.

One of the coaches forming three-set No. 103 (built in December 1909) was fitted with Vickers' lighting for comparative trials with Stone's system and the set was placed on several different train services for the next year or so. From 27th March, 1911, No. 103 was booked to work the 5.20 am Cannon Street to Westerham and 8.37 am return, but how long it remained on this working is not known. Certainly by 1914 there had been another major change in stock provision, and the Westerham through portion was using examples of the South Eastern's earliest bogie carriages, Tri-Composite No. 1893 and Brake Composite No. 1915 being specified for the 8.33 am to Cannon Street. At least the Great War was not made an excuse for discontinuing this train, which during 1915-16 was formed of a six-wheeled First, a Bogie First, Bogie Brake Composite and Bogie Tri-Composite No. 1906. As before, the stock returned on the 4.55 pm from Charing Cross, detached at Dunton Green and worked forward by the branch train.

The wartime period seems to have been uneventful as far as the branch was concerned, and the only major change was that, starting on 7th January, 1917, Sunday train services were suspended; their restoration came about on 22nd June, 1919. In October 1917 an extension of the up-side catch siding at Dunton Green was required, and Major W.L. Wreford was asked to sell the necessary land.

The branch train was three-coach, close-coupled set No. 279, given this number in 1915; the set itself is believed to have been formed in 1907, when all three coaches were converted from long buffers to close-coupling with short buffers. Steam heaters were fitted in November 1914. Set No. 279 was formed of London, Chatham & Dover Railway six-wheelers built in the mid-1890s: Second Brake No. 2927, with 24 seats, First No. 2445, 24 seats, and Third No. 3097, 50 seats. This little train was associated with the Westerham branch until the late 1920s; to haul it up and down a class 'Q' or 'Q1' 0-4-4 tank engine was normally employed.

The branch line still possessed a full complement of station masters until about 1924, when both Brasted and Westerham came under control of the Dunton Green station master. Between about 1906 and 1915 William Fright presided over Westerham, E.W. Howard was in charge of Brasted and George Edward Hayward looked after Dunton Green. By 1918 [Kelly's Directory to Kent] Mr Fright had been replaced by H.C. Trigg at Westerham, but by 1924 Frederick William Brockman, at Dunton Green, was in charge.

After the war the South Eastern & Chatham presented a very different face from the one it had had at the start. Gone were the beautiful locomotive and carriage liveries of green and lake respectively, replaced by a very dark grey with a huge white-painted number on the tank side or tender and by dark brown on carriages. Also, train fares were almost double what they had been in 1914, since all reduced fares had been abolished during the war, deliberately to discourage pleasure travel.

Punctuality was not improved in the London area, mainly because of the bad track layouts at the many junctions, and in 1921 the SE&CR announced a scheme for electrification: the system to be used differed from both those of the London, Brighton & South Coast (6,700 volts AC overhead) and the London & South Western (LSWR) (600 volts DC third rail) as it was intended that 3,000 volts DC should be fed into two conductor rails, the voltage being divided equally between the two, three-coach trains being employed. Stage Two of this scheme was to have included Orpington to Tonbridge and the Westerham branch. Nothing was done, as the influence of the LSWR was already strong and its General Manager, Sir Herbert Walker, had no wish for the future 'Southern' group of railways to be saddled with three different systems of electrification. In any case, the SE&CR had difficulty in raising the necessary capital. Whether there was economic justification for running electric trains to Westerham, whose population had increased by only 150 from 1911 to 3,200 in 1921, seems doubtful.

During 1920 Oxted tunnel, on the joint line, was closed during off-peak periods for essential repairs, and holders of SE&CR season tickets on that line were allowed to use Westerham - although the road journeys between there and Oxted were made at their own expense.

The summer timetable of 1920 had some points of interest: the through train from Westerham to Cannon Street was now booked to be worked by four-coach set No. 127 (built in 1910), a bogie Composite and, except on Saturdays, three bogie Firsts. Set 127, which was berthed at Sevenoaks, ran empty to Dunton Green to work the 7.43 am thence to Westerham hauled by a main line engine; the branch engine ran light from Dunton Green to Westerham and then worked the main line set to Dunton Green at 8.05 and back at 8.25 am. The main line engine then took over Set 127 for the 8.44 am Westerham to Cannon Street and the branch engine ran light back to Dunton Green where the branch train (Set No. 279) had been left earlier. Set No. 127 returned to Sevenoaks on the 5.05 pm from Cannon Street (not Saturdays) or 4.55 pm from Charing Cross (Saturdays); these conveyed through coaches for Westerham detached at Dunton Green and forwarded by the branch train at 5.57 pm - the bogie Composite, which remained at Westerham for attaching to the 8.44 am up next morning, and a Third and brake van which were returned to Orpington empty in the 9.15 pm goods train from Westerham to Hither Green.

Except on Wednesdays and Saturdays, the weekday branch timetable showed 13 down trains and 12 up; on Wednesdays there were two extra trains each way late at night. On Saturdays 15 trains each way were advertised. Close-coupled brake vans Nos. 160 and 516 were allotted to the branch to run with the three-coach close-coupled set No. 279. No. 516, a LC&DR vehicle, dated back to 1874.

For the summer timetable of 1922 an extra train each way ran on Mondays to Fridays and the two additional late-night trains now ran on Mondays and Thursdays (instead of Wednesdays and Saturdays), whilst the Saturday service was in consequence reduced to 14 trains each way. Light engine movements were now abolished, and the 8.18 am Dunton Green to Westerham and 8.40 am up were worked by an engine at each end of the train over the length of the branch, except on Saturdays. Logically one would expect that the main line engine remained attached at the Dunton Green end of the train (having worked

SOUTH EASTERN AND CHATHAM RAILWAY
TIMETABLE COMMENCING 4th OCTOBER, 1920

WEEK DAYS

DOWN	A am	Engine and Bke am	am	LE am	am	am	am	am	pm	pm	SO pm	pm
Dunton Green dep	4 45	..	6 47	7 30	7 43	8 25	9 32	11 2	1 8	2 18	3 25	4 5
Chevening Halt	....	....	6 50	....	7 46	8 28	9 35	11 5	1 11	2 21	3 29	4 8
Brasted	..	6 0	6 55	..	7 51	8 33	9 40	11 10	1 16	2 26	3 34	4 13
Westerham... arr	5 5	6 5	6 58	7 38	7 54	8 36	9 43	11 13	1 19	2 29	3 36	4 16

DOWN	pm	TC pm	SX pm	SO pm	SX pm	pm	WSO pm	WSO mid
Dunton Green dep	4 47	5 56	6 25	6 32	7 21	8 15	10 25	12 0
Chevening Halt	4 50	5 59	6 28	6 35	7 24	8 18	10 28	12 3
Brasted	4 55	6 4	6 33	6 40	7 29	8 24	10 33	12 8
Westerham .. arr	4 58	6 7	6 36	6 43	7 32	8 27	10 36	12 11

WEEK DAYS

UP	Goods am	am	am	am	T am	am	LE am	pm	pm	SO pm	pm	pm
Westerham .. dep	5 30	6 20	7 10	8 5	8 44	9 0	10 40	12 20	1 55	3 5	3 45	4 27
Brasted	5 35	6 23	7 13	8 8	8 47	....	10 43	12 23	1 58	3 8	3 48	4 30
Chevening Halt	..	6 27	7 17	8 12	8 51	..	10 47	12 27	2 2	3 12	3 52	4 34
Dunton Green arr	....	6 31	7 21	8 16	8 55	9 8	10 51	12 31	2 6	3 16	3 56	4 38

UP	SO pm	SX pm	LE SX pm	SO pm	SX pm	pm	B pm	WSO pm	WSO pm
Westerham .. dep	5 12	5 29	6 12	6 13	6 50	7 46	9 15	10 5	11 40
Brasted	5 15	5 32	....	6 16	6 53	7 49	9z50	10 8	11 43
Chevening Halt	5 19	5 36	..	..	6 56	7 53	..	10 12	11 47
Dunton Green arr	5 23	5 40	6 20	6 23	7 1	7 57	10 0	10 16	11 51

A—Goods 1.45 am from Hither Green Sidings.
B—Goods to Hither Green.   LE—Light Engine.
T—Through Train to Cannon Street.   TC—Through Carriages from London.
SX—Saturdays Excepted. SO—Saturdays Only.   WSO—Wednesdays and
Saturdays only.   z—Arrive 9.20 pm.

Class 'Q' 0-4-4 tank locomotive No. 420 with London, Chatham & Dover Railway carriages at Westerham in 1913. The engine was built by Neilson, Reid & Co. in 1897, rebuilt with domed boiler to 'Q1' in 1914 and withdrawn in 1927. *Historical Model Railway Society*

Westerham station from the loading dock about 1921, with branch train No. 279 ready for departure and a spare six-wheeled carriage at the end of the goods siding. The engine shed was still standing. The picture is believed to have been taken by E.T. Miller.

H.J. Patterson Rutherford Series

it empty from Sevenoaks) and the branch engine - which was attached at Dunton Green on to the 8.18 am and detached there from the 8.40 am Westerham to Cannon Street - would be at the Westerham end of the train. In the evening, the 6.48 pm (not Saturdays) from Westerham to Dunton Green was now double-headed; formerly one of the two engines had run light from Westerham to Dunton Green. The 5.57 pm Dunton Green to Westerham no longer conveyed a through portion from London on Saturdays, and the 8.45 pm goods from Westerham to Hither Green ceased to run on Saturdays.

Even the Sunday service had some points of interest. The morning trips were worked by Set 279 and the 12.32 pm from Westerham ran through to Orpington. Here it was attached to a five-coach close-coupled suburban set of London, Chatham & Dover four-wheelers (code 'ZB') and at 2.00 pm this combined train departed for Westerham. On arrival there the branch set was berthed and the 'ZB' set worked all the remaining afternoon train services finishing with the 9.05 pm Westerham to Orpington. This is the only known regular working of a suburban set south of Orpington, and presumably it was employed to provide necessary extra capacity on the branch line for tourists and hikers, who would have been unlikely to complain about the spartan comforts of four-wheeled carriage stock.

In 1922 Winston Leonard Spencer Churchill purchased Chartwell, near Westerham, and this was to be his residence until 1965. Three wagonloads of Westmoreland stone for Chartwell arrived at the station during the late 1920s, the material being used to make Churchill's rock garden and goldfish pool.

In later years at least, he never used the line, though the occasional parcel for Chartwell arrived by train. There was one regular traffic over the railway on his account, however - maggots! These were destined for Churchill's goldfish pond in the extensive grounds at Chartwell.

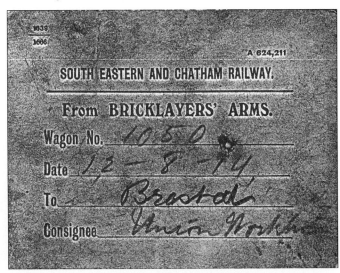

SE&CR Wagon Label.

Chapter Six

Southern Railway
1923 to 1939

From 1st January, 1923, the Westerham branch became a very small and unimportant part of the newly-created Southern Railway (SR), one of the four 'grouped' railway companies formed under the Railways Act of 1921. No overnight changes were apparent, and for a year the branch locomotive still appeared in wartime slate-grey and the carriages in brown. It was not until November 1923 that the first locomotive left Ashford Works in new Southern livery - a pleasant mid-green with black and white lining. Over the next few years more locomotives and carriages appeared on the scene in new livery.

The first major change was the abolition of second class bookings, as from September 1923; what was now styled the Eastern Section of the SR being the last to maintain them on ordinary trains. Around the same time a new range of reduced-fare tickets began to be available to try to stimulate traffic, ordinary fares having become very expensive during the recent war. Now, weekend tickets at a cost of a single fare and a third were available between any two stations by ordinary trains at or after 5.00 pm on Fridays, any train on Saturdays, for return on Sunday or Monday. The minimum fare on Saturdays had been reduced to five shillings; in practice these weekend tickets would have been of use only to passengers travelling between London and Westerham, so far as the branch was concerned. Another facility was the market ticket, issued on Saturdays by specified trains to market or shopping centres such as Sevenoaks or Tonbridge. Also announced was that parties of not less than 12 travelling to sports meetings, bazaars or picnics could, by prior arrangement, travel by ordinary train at a single fare for the return journey.

Also conveyed by passenger trains, to Westerham as just about everywhere else, were milk in churns, newspapers and perishables; and in 1923 the rates for these were substantially reduced. Judging by the number of milk churns regularly adorning the station platform at Westerham, there was still quite a heavy milk traffic. Soon the road motor would take most of it away, although the railway still retained a fair share until 1947 at least.

Timber structures, such as those at Dunton Green, Westerham and Brasted stations, needed frequent repainting if they were not to deteriorate rapidly, and by the mid-1920s they were wearing the Southern's new colours: stone (or buff) with green corner pillars, window frames and doors. Westerham's water tank and goods yard crane were light grey. At an unknown date - but certainly by 1927 - the window at the south-west elevation of the station building was taken out and the gap panelled over in matching style, a lean-to wooden hut for stores being erected there. The engine shed is stated to have been closed in 1925 and it was demolished soon afterwards.

The former SER classes 'Q' and 'Q1' 0-4-4 tank locomotives were still to be seen on the branch until 1927 or 1928, and D.L. Bradley has recorded that 'Q' Nos. 26 and 173 and 'Q1' Nos. 355, 404 and 416 were transferred to Tonbridge in 1925, one being used on the Dunton Green-Westerham service [*Locomotives of*

Class 'B' 4-4-0 locomotive No. A458, never rebuilt to 'B1', at Westerham with (presumably) Set 655, three ex-LC&DR six-wheeled carriages, 12th November, 1927.

H.C. Casserley

the South Eastern Railway, page 9]. All were withdrawn between 1926 and 1928, being replaced on the branch by Stirling 4-4-0 or 0-6-0 tender locomotives, despite the lack of turntables. Class 'O1' No. A123 of Tonbridge is stated to have been a frequent performer on the branch between 1929 and 1932.

Until about 1933 locomotives from both Bricklayers Arms and Tonbridge had regular duties on the branch. It seems likely that the Bricklayers Arms engine (the last 'B', or 'B1' or 'O1') came down with the 2.45 am freight from Hither Green sidings to Westerham (due 5.10 am) and worked the morning passenger services. The 8.22 am Dunton Green to Westerham and 8.40 am up were worked by an engine at each end of the train; the 8.40 am continued to Charing Cross after the rear engine had come off at Dunton Green. Presumably the Bricklayers Arms engine continued with the branch service until midday, going to Tonbridge for servicing, and then returned in time to take the 9.05 pm freight from Westerham to Chislehurst. A relieving Tonbridge 4-4-0 or 'O1' 0-6-0 would have come up to work most of the afternoon and evening passenger service on the branch.

On Sundays in 1927 a light engine ran from Tonbridge to Westerham in order to take out the 7.20 am to Dunton Green; the 1.12 and 9.00 pm were through trains from Westerham to Orpington, balanced by the 3.45 and 9.45 pm Orpington to Westerham. After working the last down train of the day, the engine berthed the carriages and returned light from Westerham to Tonbridge.

Few people would have witnessed the bizarre spectacle of a goods brake van being propelled cautiously from Brasted to Westerham early every morning, but nevertheless it was a regular event. Upon arrival of the morning freight at Westerham its locomotive ran round the wagons and took any required for Brasted back up the line again, leaving at 5.25 am. After 15 minutes allowed for shunting and setting down wagons at Brasted sidings the 'train' left for Westerham, guard's van leading, at 5.45; for the 1¾-mile journey in this direction 11 minutes were allowed.

During the whole of the 1920s the regular branch train was SE&CR No. 279 (SR No. 655), a three-coach set of close-coupled former London, Chatham & Dover six-wheeled carriages: a Second Brake (re-classified Third Brake from September 1923), a First and a Third. Set 655 was repainted in Southern green, with yellow and black lining and class letters on the doors in place of the large serifed figures used by the SE&C, in March 1927. Unlike other similar three-coach sets it was not fitted for push-and-pull working. Withdrawal came about in November 1929. After this, for a couple of years, a former London, Brighton & South Coast Railway bogie Composite, with three first-class and four third-class compartments, working with a former SE&C six-wheeled passenger guard's van, made up the normal branch train. If a single coach was all that was required by 1930 passenger traffic must have been already very light; however, on Whit Monday 9th June, 1930, the operating department did manage to find an extra bogie Composite to carry the expected additional passengers. In fact it was Rotherhithe Road (Bermondsey) carriage depot which was responsible for the provision of stock on the branch, and when carriages were exchanged for maintenance they were forwarded by van trains normally, although as a last resort they could be attached to passenger trains.

Typical Vale of Holmesdale scenery on the branch seen from one of the bridges between Chevening and Brasted. Class 'B1' 4-4-0 No. A451 of Tonbridge is working a Westerham to Dunton Green train on 24th April, 1930.   *R.W. Kidner*

As one arrived at Westerham station from the town centre one might be lucky enough to see class 'B1' 4-4-0 No. A451 apparently sprouting in a cabbage patch but actually running round its train. Also visible are the oil-store (a corrugated-iron hut), a pile of bricks awaiting collection, and the offices of Openshaw the coal merchants in this view recorded on 24th April, 1930.

R.W. Kidner

The other regular set working on the branch was that used for the through train to Cannon Street (SE&CR No. 127, which from 1924 was renumbered SR No. 674). This four-coach bogie set had been built in 1910, so was still relatively modern; it worked with two 'loose' bogie Firsts and was berthed overnight at Sevenoaks. The February 1926 carriage working book shows that Set 674, plus two Firsts, ran empty from Sevenoaks to Dunton Green at 8.00 am, forming the 8.10 am to Westerham; it then left for Cannon Street at 8.40 am. The branch enjoyed no balancing down through train as the set returned to Sevenoaks direct, by the 5.08 (not Saturdays) from Cannon Street or the 7.10 pm (Saturdays) from Charing Cross. From 11th July, 1926, there was a change in the down working, for Set 674 was now on the 4.30 pm (not Saturdays) from Charing Cross to Sevenoaks and on Saturdays the 2.04 pm Cannon Street to Wadhurst; because of this the empty train on Monday mornings had to start from Tonbridge instead of Sevenoaks.

Set 674 was still used for Westerham's through train in 1931/2, by then working with a loose First, a Composite with four first-class and three third-class compartments, and a brake van. Running empty from Sevenoaks to Dunton Green, this formation then worked the 8.15 am to Westerham and 8.38 am thence to Cannon Street. The evening return service to Sevenoaks, except on Saturdays, was the 6.25 pm from Charing Cross, and on Saturdays Set 674 was on the 1.06 pm Cannon Street to Tunbridge Wells, thence empty to Sevenoaks. Unfortunately the luxury of a through train was destined not to last beyond 1933, with the exception of a few trains running to and from Orpington.

During this period the branch passenger train service still contrived to be 'unbalanced': the Monday-to-Friday table for summer 1927 showed 16 down and 15 up trains, with two extra late-evening trains each way on Wednesdays; by summer 1930 an extra peak-hour train each way had been slotted in, so that there were now 17 down and 16 up trains, plus the two extras each way on Wednesday nights. Saturday service between 1927 and 1930 remained at 16 trains each way. It is not at all clear how the extra down train, the 5.58 pm (Saturdays excepted) from Dunton Green, was 'balanced'. Stock for the following train, the 6.26 pm from Dunton Green, came empty from Sevenoaks on Mondays to Fridays, and either one or the other must have returned to the junction, combined with one of the passenger trains or perhaps with the 9.05 pm freight.

The Sunday service of 11 trains each way seemed to have been geared to the requirements of day-trippers, with a reasonable service in the morning and from the late afternoon but nothing for four hours after lunch.

The freight service in summer 1930 was similar to that provided three years earlier: 2.45 am Hither Green to Westerham: 5.15 am Westerham to Brasted and 5.35 am return (brake van propelled); and 8.50 pm Westerham to Chislehurst.

One result of the use of large-wheeled tender engines on the passenger trains was an increase in the running time from 11 minutes in 1927 to 13 minutes by 1930. Tender-first running was most uncomfortable for engine crews as they were exposed to the westerly gales, or sometimes the easterly ones, as well as the various sorts of precipitation - although it was sometimes possible to fit up a crude weatherboard or stormsheet.

A strengthened branch train for Whit Monday, 9th June, 1930, enters Chevening Halt, headed by class 'O1' No. A426.   *R.W. Kidner*

The same train has entered Chevening Halt, which still had its sleeper-built platform. Nothing much is happening here, but two passengers have spotted the photographer. The train comprised an ex-SE&CR six-wheeled brake van and the two ex-LBSCR bogie coaches.

R.W. Kidner

The branch line and its trains held a great charm for those persons who studied railways, and a frequent visitor between 1930 and 1933 was Mr R.W. Kidner, who found the branch to be an ideal item in a bicycle tour from his home in Sidcup, taking in a favourite bridge by Polhill Intermediate signal cabin on the main line and Sevenoaks Bat & Ball engine shed. These were the engines he noted on the Westerham branch, usually on afternoon workings:

'B1'	A451	(Tonbridge)	24th April, 1930
'B1'	A444	(Tonbridge)	8th June, 1930
'O1'	A426	(Bricklayers Arms?)	9th June, 1930
'B1'	A440	(Bricklayers Arms)	4th November, 1930
'O1'	A429	(Tonbridge)	30th April, 1931
'O1'	A251	(Bricklayers Arms)	25th April, 1932
'O1'	1048	(Tonbridge)	15th April, 1933

'The view from the station road at Westerham of the 'F1', 'B1' or 'O1' engine running round its single coach in what appeared to be a cabbage patch was one of the minor pleasures of the early thirties,' wrote Mr Kidner in 1976 (*Southern Railway Branch Lines in the Thirties*). Quite true: there was a small vegetable plot between the south-west end of the station building, the road, and the track.

The celebrated H.C. Casserley had already paid his first visit to Westerham on 12th November 1927, where he was lucky enough to see one of the last two Stirling class 'B' locomotives with domeless boiler, No. A458 on the three-coach six-wheeled set.

Just over a month later the tranquillity of the branch was upset by a very severe snowstorm which fell on the country on Boxing Day, 1927. The line was blocked and indeed the villages around Westerham were isolated for some weeks. When the snow melted there were floods, and during January 1928 some houses in Westerham and Brasted were damaged by floodwater. Train services were disrupted, and the SR printed a notice for display in the affected areas:

SOUTHERN RAILWAY

29th December, 1927

In consequence of snow drifts, floods etc., intending passengers should he warned that delays to services will occur and that owing to the undermentioned lines being blocked, no service can be guaranteed to stations on those lines.
Westerham branch. Dyke branch. Hurstbourne and Longparish.
Between Alton and Winchester. Basingstoke and Alton branch.

Until 1926 the station master responsible for both Dunton Green and Westerham was Frederick William Brockman. As previously mentioned, since about 1924 the whole branch line had been put under the control of the Dunton Green station master, this being Albert William Beck from 1927 until 1935; Mr J.H. Wildish replaced him in 1936.

When the signal cabin on the up platform at Dunton Green had been replaced by a new one on the down side it presented a difficulty with regard to tablet exchange between the signalman and engineman. An aerial ropeway to carry

The normal branch train of the early 1930s: class 'O1' 0-6-0 No. A429 of Tonbridge with an afternoon departure from Dunton Green on 30th April, 1931. One of the goods sidings south of the station appears to be occupied by spare carriages.   *R.W. Kidner*

Chevening Halt, from the road bridge, showing the usual one-coach train, but with an ex-LC&DR six-wheeled brake van, whose guard is giving the 'right away' on 16th September, 1931.
R.W. Kidner

the tablet was therefore erected between the signal cabin and the north end of the up platform, right across the main line and sufficiently clear of the headroom. On the up platform there was a wooden ramp, at the top of which the engineman could surrender or collect the tablet. From the Central-Eastern Appendix to the Working Timetables dated 26th March, 1934, are quoted the following instructions:

DUNTON GREEN

Custody and transference of electric train tablet. - The Guard of a train working to and from Westerham is authorised to carry out the duty of delivering the tablet to or receiving it from the Driver at Dunton Green. He will also take the tablet from the aerial carrier or deposit it therein for transmission to the Signalman.

In the case of a pull and push train working without a Guard an adult member of the Dunton Green staff is authorised to carry out these duties. When an empty pull and push train or an engine is running on this branch and no member of the platform staff is available at Dunton Green, these duties will be carried out by the Fireman.

Push-and-pull working on the Westerham branch appears to have been inaugurated in September 1931, with Set 758 - a former London, Brighton & South Coast Railway 'air-control' two-coach set - booked as the regular train. It was berthed at Sevenoaks, and worked the branch during the evening, starting with the 4.35 pm (not Saturdays) or 4.14 pm (Saturdays), until 'close of play', the 10.20 pm (not Wednesdays) or 12.30 am (Wednesdays) from Dunton Green to Westerham. The set then returned empty from Westerham.

Also during this period an ex-LB&SC Brake Composite, No. 6924, was scheduled to work the branch, being berthed at the terminus. Starting with the first up train it formed every train until the 4.00 pm (not Saturdays) or 3.31 pm (Saturdays) from Westerham to Dunton Green - except the through train to London and its previous working, the 8.15 am Dunton Green to Westerham. The loose Brake Composite finished its day with the 6.24 pm (not Saturdays) or 5.20 pm (Saturdays) from Dunton Green to Westerham.

On Sundays from September 1931 this carriage was booked to work all trains, including three through to Orpington at 8.10 am, 1.30 and 9.40 pm from Westerham; an empty train from Orpington to Dunton Green at 8.55 am, thence passenger to Westerham, and two through workings at 3.37 and 10.38 pm. There is some doubt as to whether these down trains were available to the public as through trains; as the stock had to be shunted across from the down platform to the branch platform at Dunton Green it may be that passengers had to 'change', walk across the footbridge, and board the train from which they had just alighted. Some of the waits of down trains at that station were quite lengthy, and *Bradshaw* did not advertise the trains as through; but the carriage working notice indicated that as far as stock working was concerned there were three trains each way between Westerham and Orpington on Sundays.

The late-night Wednesday trains added to the complications of timetabling. In the summer 1932 timetable the push-and-pull set that worked the evening branch service normally returned to Tonbridge empty from Westerham at 10.49

SOUTHERN RAILWAY

TIMETABLE COMMENCING 16th JULY, 1933

DOWN — WEEK DAYS

	Freight 3.45 am Sevenoaks	Engine and Bke		*					SO	SO	SO
	am	am	am	am	am	am	am	am	pm	pm	pm
Dunton Green dep	4 30	..	6 33	7 20	8 15	9 2	10 17	11 0	12 26	1 17	2 8
Chevening Halt	....	....	6 36	....	....	9 5	10 20	11 3	12 29	1 20	2 11
Brasted	..	5 35	6 41½	7 26½	8 22½	9 10½	10 25½	11 8½	12 34½	1 25½	2 16½
Westerham ...arr	4 50	5 46	6 46	7 31	8 27	9 15	10 30	11 13	12 39	1 30	2 21

DOWN	SO	* SO	* NS	*	* NS	NS	* SO	* NS	SO	NS		SO
	pm	pm	pm	pm	pm	pm	pm	pm	pm	pm	pm	pm
Dunton Green dep	3 6	4 14	4 35	5 20	5 55	6 20	6 24	6 54	7 36	7 47	8 29	10 30
Chevening Halt	3 8	4 17	4 38	5 23	5 58	6 23	6 27	6 57	7 39	7 50	8 32	10 33
Brasted	3 14½	4 22½	4 43½	5 28½	6 3½	6 28½	6 32½	7 2½	7 44½	7 55½	8 37½	10 39½
Westerham .. arr	3 19	4 27	4 48	5 33	6 8	6 33	6 37	7 7	7 49	8 0	8 42	10 44

SUNDAYS

DOWN				11.34 am Orpington		1.49 pm Orpington	4.10 pm Orpington						10.40 pm Orpington
	am	am	am	am	pm	pm	pm	pm	pm	pm	pm	pm	pm
Dunton Grn dep	7† 0	7 50	10 2	11 50	12 40	2 7	4 29	5 35	6 35	7 19	8 0	9 0	11 4
Chevening Halt	....	7 53	10 5	11 53	12 43	2 10	4 32	5 38	6 38	7 22	8 3	9 3	11 7
Brasted	..	7 58½	10 10½	11 58½	12 48½	2 15½	4 37½	5 43½	6 43½	7 27½	8 8½	9 8½	11 12½
Westerham arr	7†12	8 3	10 15	12 3	12 53	2 20	4 42	5 48	6 48	7 32	8 13	9 13	11 17

UP — WEEK DAYS

	Freight			* G				SO	SO	SO	SO	SO
	am	am	am	am	am	am	am	noon	pm	pm	pm	pm
Westerham .. dep	5 15	6 10	7 1	7 45	8 40	9 58	10 40	12 0	12 58	1 39	2 45	3 30
Brasted	5 20	6 14	7 5	7 49	8 44	10 2	10 44	12 4	1 2	1 43	2 49	3 34
Chevening Halt	..	6 19	7 10	7 54	8 49	10 7	10 49	12 9	1 7	1 48	2 54	3 39
Dunton Green arr	....	6 23	7 14	7 58	8 53	10 11	10 53	12 13	1 11	1 52	2 58	3 43

UP	*	* NS	* SO	* NS	* B	NS		Freight to Hither Green SO	Freight to Hither Green NS	SO
	pm	pm	pm	pm	pm	pm	pm	pm	pm	pm
Westerham .. dep	4 53	5 38	6 5	6 40	7 15	7 31	8 10	8 50	9 5	9 40
Brasted	4 57	5 42	6 9	....	7 19	....	8 14	9z10	9z25	9 44
Chevening Halt	5 2	5 47	6 14	..	7 24	..	8 19	...	..	9 49
Dunton Green arr	5 6	5 51	6 18	6 50	7 28	7 41	8 23	9 20	9 35	9 53

SUNDAYS

UP		G			G	G						G	D
	am	am	am	pm	pm	pm	pm	pm	pm	pm	pm	pm	pm
Westerham dep	7 28	8 12	10 25	12 18	1 0	2 27	5 11	6 13	7 0	7 41	8 28	9 40	11‖25
Brasted	7 32	8 16	10 29	12 22	1 4	2 31	5 15	6 17	7 4	7 45	8 32	9 44	....
Chevening Halt	7 37	8 21	10 34	12 27	1 9	2 36	5 20	6 22	7 9	7 50	8 37	9 49	..
Dunton Grn arr	7 41	8 25	10 38	12 31	1 13	2 40	5 24	6 26	7 13	7 54	8 41	9 53	11‖35

* - Pull and Push Train. B-To Bromley South. D-To Tonbridge.
G-To Orpington. NS-Not Saturdays. SO-Saturdays only.
z-Arrive 15 minutes earlier. ‖-Light Engine. †-Empty Train.

pm. On Wednesdays this was replaced by a 10.49 pm passenger train to Dunton Green, returning thence at 11.27 pm and forming the 11.45 pm Westerham to Dunton Green. It continued empty to Orpington to form the 12.15 am (Wednesday night/Thursday morning) through train to Westerham, due 12.46 am, and finally ran thence empty to Tonbridge.

All these late Wednesday trains were discontinued in September 1932, and another loss at this time was the entire train service in the middle of the day, Mondays to Fridays, the last morning down train being the 11.00 am from Dunton Green and the first one of the afternoon the 4.35 pm (not Saturdays). The early 1930s were not a good time for the railways; there was less money about, a depressed economy, and branch lines were beginning to be shed from the network. The Westerham line's traffic was undoubtedly being lost, but presumably not to such an extent as to warrant complete closure at this stage; the Southern Railway had no desire to close any line that was not absolutely hopeless.

The train service for September 1932 showed six up and down trains in the morning; the Monday-to-Friday afternoon service comprised six down and four up trains, the last being the 8.28 pm from Dunton Green to Westerham. There were some very tight connections at Dunton Green for up trains, the 7.33 am from Westerham for instance having only one minute for the change.

In the evening the 5.30 pm from Charing Cross called at Dunton Green 50 minutes later, giving a four-minute connection with the 6.24 pm to Westerham. The 6.30 pm from Charing Cross also gave a four-minute connection into the 7.21 pm Dunton Green to Westerham. The 4.03 pm from Orpington terminated at Dunton Green and after 17 minutes, during which time it shunted to the branch platform, formed the 4.35 pm to Westerham.

There were several changes to the timetable that began on Sunday 16th July, 1933. The through train from Westerham to Cannon Street ran for the last time on the 15th, and from the 17th the 8.40 am now terminated at Dunton Green, passengers changing into a new fast train that had left Ashford at 7.34 am for Cannon Street, where it was due at 9.24 am. As compensation, this was several minutes faster for Westerham passengers than the through train had been.

A push-and-pull set left Sevenoaks empty for Dunton Green, forming the 7.20 am to Westerham and the 7.45 am through train to Orpington, replacing the 7.33 am from Westerham. The 7.01 am Westerham to Dunton Green continued as an empty train to Knockholt, and the rest of the morning services on the branch were provided by a train that had started from Ashford at 6.50 am (due Dunton Green 8.04 am), beginning with the 8.15 am Dunton Green to Westerham.

The evening service, Mondays to Fridays, was improved slightly with one extra down and two extra up trains, and there was virtually a half-hourly interval service between 5.20 and 6.54 pm, mostly provided by a push-and-pull set. This had come from Orpington at 4.03 pm (not Saturdays), beginning work on the branch with the 4.35 pm to Westerham, and ran four return trips of which the last, the 7.15 pm from Westerham, was a through train to Orpington and Bromley South. On Saturdays the push-and-pull set ran empty from Sevenoaks to take up the working with the 4.14 pm Dunton Green to

A Westerham train at Brasted, 15th April, 1933, with class 'OI' 0-6-0 locomotive No. 1048 of Tonbridge and ex-LBSCR two-coach set (recently reduced from three coaches). The enamelled advertisement 'Ovum for Poultry' and the station name in whitewashed stones (*left*) were features of this station during the 1930s.

C.R. Gordon Stuart

Westerham, did three return trips and left the branch on the 7.15 pm Westerham to Bromley South. The 6.20 pm (not Saturdays) was an 'extra' train, not worked by the push-and-pull set, and the rest of the evening's services after 7.30 pm were also worked by ordinary trains. In total there were 13 down and 12 up trains, Mondays to Fridays, and 16 trains each way on Saturdays.

The Sunday service was stepped up to 12 trains each way and there were now five trains running through to Orpington on that day. These left Westerham at 8.12, 10.25 am, 1.00, 2.27 and 9.40 pm; through stock workings returned from Orpington to Westerham at 11.34 am, 1.49, 4.10 and 10. 40 pm.

The goods service was revised also. The morning train now left Sevenoaks at 3.45 am and Dunton Green 4.30 am. Brasted wagons were taken on a trip from Westerham at 5.15 am, the brake van returning at 5.35 am. The evening freight left Westerham at 9.05 pm (not Saturdays) or 8.50 pm (Saturdays). Fifteen minutes were allowed at Brasted to pick up wagons, and from Dunton Green the train continued to Hither Green.

In September 1933 a new locomotive shed at Hither Green was opened and for the next two years this was responsible for providing the branch engines. Tender locomotives were no longer seen, and former London, Chatham & Dover Railway class 'R1' 0-4-4 tank engines Nos. 1700 and 1704, fitted with air-control apparatus, began to take charge, working two-coach push-and-pull sets. However, Tonbridge Shed still had a hand in the working, class 'H' No. 1324 being recorded on 16th June, 1934. For working with such engines as these, which were not at that time fitted for working push-and-pull trains, there were some two-coach sets of ex-London, Brighton & South Coast (LB&SCR) stock formed of a five-compartment Third Brake and a Composite which had originally been three-coach 'Rover' sets.

The Southern announced in December 1933 its plans for further electrification and, during 1934, conductor rails were laid between Orpington and Sevenoaks, with the intention that the existing local electric service between London and Orpington should be extended to Sevenoaks. As there were fears that, should the aerial tablet carrier at Dunton Green break and fall across the tracks, it would cause a short circuit, it ceased to be used on and from 16th September, 1934. Henceforth, the single line instruments were kept in a small enclosure on the branch platform.

Push-and-pull trains on certain branch lines of the Southern Railway were authorised to be worked without a guard in the 1930s. Instructions for the working of such trains on the Westerham branch appeared in the SR's Central-Eastern Appendix to the Working Timetables for 26th March, 1934:

A junior Porter will accompany the train to issue and collect tickets as far as this may be necessary at Chevening Halt and at Brasted, and to perform the work of platform Porter at those places where the train is booked to call but no platform staff are on duty.

The junior Porter will also be responsible at such places for giving the signal to the Driver to indicate when the platform work is completed and all is right for the train to proceed. He will undertake no responsibility appertaining to the actual running of the train.

When Pull and Push trains are worked without a Guard between Westerham and Dunton Green, and the engine is propelling, an exchange of bell signals, viz., two rings,

An Orpington to Westerham push-and-pull with 'R1' class 0-4-4T, seen in delightful scenery near Brasted on 5th May, 1934.   *L.T. Catchpole*

An early evening view of Westerham station with push-and-pull set No. 481 on 16th June, 1934.
H.C. Casserley

must be made between the Driver and Fireman 200 yards from Brasted Station, Chevening Halt and up home signal at Dunton Green. In the absence of a bell signal from the Driver, the Fireman must be prepared to bring the train to a stand at the signal, station or halt platform, as the case may be.

As no mention is made of trains working with an engine at each end on the branch, it is assumed that this practice was given up when the through train to London was discontinued.

The 'economy' train service ran until January 1935, when the entire timetable was recast owing to the electrification of the main line.

Population of Brasted was only 1,379 and of Westerham 3,368 in 1931. What sorts of tickets were residents able to purchase during the early 1930s? There was quite a wide range, apart from Ordinary Singles, which were quite expensive. Summer Returns, at the rate of 1d. per mile, were available any day by any train between any two stations for return within one month. Weekend Returns were available on Fridays after 4.00 am, Saturdays and Sundays, for return on Saturdays, Sundays, Mondays and Tuesdays the same weekend. Cheap Day Returns were available from London daily by any train, and to London by any train from 9.30 am on weekdays and without restriction Sundays and Bank Holidays.

Fares for July 1934 were as under:

	Ticket	Brasted		Westerham	
		1st	3rd	1st	3rd
Charing Cross	Single	5s. 0d.	3s. 0d.	5s. 4d.	3s. 2d.
Cannon Street	Single	4s. 9d.	2s. 10d.	5s. 2d.	3s. 0d.
London Bridge	Single	4s. 7d.	2s. 8d.	4s. 11d.	2s. 10d.
London	Summer Return	8s. 6d.	5s. 0d.	8s. 6d.	5s. 0d.
London	Weekend Return	7s. 0d.	4s. 3d.	7s. 0d.	4s. 3d.
London	Cheap Day	5s. 3d.	3s. 1d.	5s. 3d.	3s. 1d.

It may be seen that Cheap Day tickets cost little more than the Ordinary Singles. The 9.58 am from Westerham was the first train on weekdays on which they could be used.

An opportunity was missed to electrify the Westerham branch at the time of the Sevenoaks scheme, but presumably a decision had been taken that the amount of traffic on the line did not warrant it. There were other short lines with little traffic prospects that received the conductor rail, usually because it was found expedient to terminate electric trains at the end of a branch rather than on the main line (an example being Haywards Heath to Horsted Keynes). But Westerham did not seem to fit into this category - the Southern wished to provide Sevenoaks with a half-hourly service of electric trains and it would have been undesirable to give Knockholt and Dunton Green two trains an hour, only to divert one per hour to Westerham instead of Sevenoaks. The SR Board was usually very careful about committing itself to capital expenditure when there was little prospect of a return but, had the branch been converted and the junction altered to facilitate the working of through trains, house-building would undoubtedly have followed and the hopes of the promoters, back in

1881, would at last have been realised. As it was, the branch remained steam-operated, the valley was not built on, and traffic continued to be light.

A cheaper way of trying to stimulate traffic on the branch was to run push-and-pull trains to a greatly improved timetable, and so this is what happened as from Sunday 6th January, 1935, the day electric train services on the main line began running to the new timetable. The branch train now ran hourly during the middle of the day (Mondays to Fridays) and in the late afternoons (Saturdays) and late evenings, and also all day on Sundays. Connections were therefore made at Dunton Green with alternate electric trains. The peak service was still irregular and on Saturdays covered lunchtime and early afternoon with the result that few trains ran at the same times as they did on Mondays to Fridays. The entire train service was operated by push-and-pull trains; there were 22 down trains plus a late-night Wednesday train, and 21 up. The branch engine arrived on the 2.40 am freight from Hither Green (due Westerham 4.35 am) took trucks to Brasted at 5.05 and returned with the brake van (propelled) 30 minutes later. The evening freight left Westerham after the last down passenger train had arrived: at 11.35 pm except on Wednesdays and at 12.50 am on Thursday mornings because of the additional Wednesday-night down passenger train, which was due in at 12.36 am.

Whether the Hither Green engine was relieved by one from Tonbridge some time during the day is not known, but it seems likely as the intensive service would not have given much time for coaling-up at Westerham - although it is said that coaling facilities remained long after the engine shed was closed.

The regular push-and-pull set now used on the branch was No. 481, which had been transferred from Swanley-Sevenoaks/Swanley-Gravesend West Street services in about May or June 1934. Set 481 and its companion, No. 482, had started life as four steam railmotors on the SE&CR in 1906 but had been converted to two-coach sets in 1924. One Brake Third in each set was retained as such, with a compartment for the driver, but the other Brake Third was converted into a Composite with a first-class saloon, and a first-class compartment where the brake-end had been. In addition the two coaches were corridor-connected. Seating capacity of each two-coach set was 15 1st class and 88 3rd class, of which 56 were in the Third Brake and 32 in the Composite. The 1st class saloon had a longitudinal seat for three passengers each side and an 'armchair' in each corner. The low-backed 3rd class seats were not very comfortable. All seating, except for the five-seat first-class compartment, was in open saloons, ideal conditions for the guard to issue tickets and, no doubt, to indulge in friendly conversation with regular passengers. These two push-and-pull trains, with their unusual feature of inward-opening external doors to the entry vestibules, were to be associated with the Westerham branch with scarcely a break until 1959.

Other types of push-and-pull trains were to be seen, however, and the ex-LB&SCR ones often put in an appearance, as well as a type that had been adapted by the SR from former AC electric stock and whose origins were betrayed by their having two windows in the drive-end vehicle instead of the usual four.

Of the locomotives in use on the line class 'R1' Nos. 1700 and 1704 were frequent performers; the first of these was transferred to Tonbridge Shed in

1935, the second in 1938. Ex-LB&SCR class 'D1/M' (motor fitted) 0-4-2 tank locomotive No. 2355, also at Tonbridge, appeared regularly from 1936 onwards, and No. 2224 of the same class was noted a year later.

In 1935 Mr A. Gurney-Smith, a regular contributor to *The Railway Magazine*, sought general support for his proposal to extend the Westerham branch eastwards under the main line at Dunton Green across to Otford Junction, on the Swanley-Sevenoaks line, in order to allow the running of a direct service of trains between Westerham and Maidstone. He thought it was lamentable that the county town of Kent should be so inaccessible from the Sevenoaks area. But, despite the fact that the recent electrification was encouraging the building of houses in the district, the general opinion was that such a service could not possibly pay, and no more was heard of it. Fifty years later the journey between the two places was facilitated - but by road, not rail.

Still seeking ways of reducing costs on the branch line, the Southern next tried out the Sentinel-Cammell Special Rail Bus. This remarkable vehicle, which had been built in 1933 and numbered 6 in the SR's railcar list, had been designed for use on the Devil's Dyke branch near Brighton. But, because it was high-geared to enable it to work at the same speed as the electric trains between Brighton and the junction near Aldrington, it could not climb the steep gradients on the Dyke branch satisfactorily and moreover its brakes proved too feeble on the downhill return trips.

The railbus, which seated only 44 passengers in two saloons divided by a central entry vestibule, had a vertical boiler of the same type as that used in Sentinel's road waggons, and it supplied steam to a 97 hp two-cylinder compound engine, nose-suspended and geared to drive only one axle. Automatic stoking was a feature that enabled the bus to be driven by one man. Slung below the floor was a 240-gallon water tank and an electric lighting battery. Braking was on separate drums fixed to the outside of the wheels. The vehicle's body, which was built by Metropolitan-Cammell and owed more to contemporary road bus design than to railway carriage, featured stylish tapered ends, and four drop lights and two oval windows each side.

After a couple of years' experience in running this experimental vehicle, the Southern decided not to purchase any more. It was the same problem that was to face British Railways many years later with their railbuses: a vehicle intended for lightly-trafficked lines, and which cannot haul a tail-load, becomes so popular that traffic is increased beyond the capacity of the vehicle.

No. 6 suffered from these defects and was taken off the Dyke branch in May 1935. On 17th October, 1935, a special trial run from Tonbridge to Westerham and back was made, calling at all stations. Leaving Tonbridge at 10.40 am, it reached Dunton Green 20 minutes later, reversal taking 10 minutes; the journey on the branch took just 11 minutes. The return trip, which left Westerham at 12.08 pm, took 12½ minutes, but after only five minutes at Dunton Green No. 6 was away again and, 17 minutes later, it was back in Tonbridge. The trial run must have proved satisfactory for, on 2nd March, 1936, No. 6 was formally transferred to the London East Division and placed into passenger service on the Westerham branch which, being easily graded, was much more suitable than the Dyke branch had been. To show its capabilities to the best advantage

Sentinel railbus No. 6 at Dunton Green working the Westerham branch service on 21st March, 1936.   *R.W. Kidner*

The only known photograph of the Sentinel railbus actually working on the Westerham branch: here shown leaving the terminus on an early evening working on 28th March, 1936.
R.W. Kidner

the journey time was reduced from 13 to 10 minutes, while at the same time train services not booked to be worked by the railbus were accelerated to 11½ minutes each way.

On weekdays the Sentinel came up from Tonbridge on the 7.23 am to Dunton Green and took over from the push-and-pull train that had worked the early-morning branch services; then, at 2.12 pm (Saturdays excepted) or 1.13 pm (Saturdays only) it ran back to Tonbridge for fire-dropping. Trains in the afternoon were again in the hands of an 'R1' or 'D1' with push-and-pull set, then at 5.00 pm the Sentinel worked 'passenger' back from Tonbridge to Dunton Green to work Westerham services for the rest of the evening, assisted by a push-and-pull train during the tea-time 'rush' when two trains were required on the line. On Sundays all services were worked by ordinary trains.

The railbus had several shortcomings. Its driver's compartment was cramped and hot, and the passenger saloons, thanks to the feeble radiators, were cold in winter. The seating capacity of 44 was somewhat inadequate for the peak periods, and there was no first class accommodation - although, somewhat illogically, the ordinary trains working on the branch retained it. First class season ticket holders travelling to and from London had to choose their trains carefully if they wished to get what they had paid for.

R.W. Kidner managed a ride in No. 6 on the 4.55 pm (SO) from Tonbridge to Dunton Green and found it 'a bit bumpy'. However, in *A Short History of Mechanical Traction and Travel* (Oakwood Press, 1947) he wrote :

This was a mettlesome vehicle, and did some very fast running in service between Tonbridge and Dunton Green. It broke down fairly frequently, however, and was a bugbear to the traffic people, as it could not handle tail traffic.

One failure in service was reported in the *Sevenoaks News* for 24th April, 1936. Three days earlier, while working the 10.52 am from Westerham, No. 6 developed engine trouble shortly after it had left Brasted station. The bus was pushed back to the station (by the passengers?). The 12 passengers, who were delayed nearly half an hour, were taken to Dunton Green by a Green Line coach. The newspaper does not say how the rest of the day's train services were operated.

The Sentinel does not seem to have been used on the Westerham branch after October 1936, and, following more failures, it was taken out of service in April 1937, although not actually broken up until 1946. Branch services reverted to being worked entirely by push-and-pull trains, and it could be said that yet another interesting experiment in economical train working had failed.

In June 1938 class 'R1' 0-4-4 tank locomotive No. 1704 was transferred from Hither Green to Tonbridge, and No. 1710 of the same class arrived there from Maidstone. Tonbridge's allocation of push-and-pull fitted engines of this type was now Nos. 1700, 1703, 1704, 1707 and 1710. The last-numbered did not long remain there, and No. 1703 went to Ashford; the allocation in August 1939 was five class 'R' (Nos. 1666/68/ 69/70/75) and three class 'R1' locomotives (Nos. 1700/04/07).

The timetable for summer 1938 showed 22 trains each way, Saturdays excepted, with an extra late-evening down train on Wednesdays; 21 trains each

A push-and-pull train for Westerham, which has just passed under the easternmost of the three overbridges between Chevening and Brasted on 3rd October, 1936; class 'D1/M' 0-4-2 tank locomotive No. 2355 and the carriages were of LB&SCR origin.   *H.C. Casserley*

Brasted station in less favourable weather: class 'D1/M' No. 2355 is seen again, this time with a push-and-pull set assembled from one ex-LB&SCR driving trailer and one ex-LSWR trailer Third. Engine duty numbers on the Eastern Section were not displayed until 1936, by which time only Set 649 had the formation shown, and this set was withdrawn in August 1937.
                                                                    Lens of Sutton

way on Saturdays; and on Sundays there were 18 down and 17 up trains. Goods traffic included domestic coal, handled by the Westerham merchants G. Alderson & Son; agricultural produce; timber; and pipes, presumably made by the brick and pottery works in London Road, Westerham. Photographs of the period show stacks of these short pipe sections by the goods shed at Westerham.

Some first class fares had been reduced since 1934, although third class fares were generally the same, except for the day return, which had increased slightly.

	Ticket	Brasted		Westerham	
		1st	3rd	1st	3rd
Charing Cross	Single	5s. 0d.	3s. 0d.	5s. 4d.	3s. 2d.
Cannon Street	Single	4s. 9d.	2s. 10d.	5s. 2d.	3s. 0d.
London Bridge	Single	4s. 7d.	2s. 8d.	4s. 11d.	2s. 10d.
London	Monthly Return	7s. 6d.	5s. 0d.	7s. 6d.	5s. 0d.
London	Weekend Return	6s. 6d.	4s. 3d.	6s. 6d.	4s. 3d.
London	Day return	5s. 0d.	3s. 3d.	5s. 3d.	3s. 3d.

Season ticket rates also were quoted in the SR suburban timetable for July 1938. The third class weekly season to Cannon Street from Chevening was 11s. 6d., from Brasted 12s. 3d. and from Westerham 12s. 9d. Dogs, accompanied or unaccompanied between London and any branch station, cost their owner 1s. 4d. for each journey. Passengers could send their luggage in advance, there being flat rates of 2s. per package (collection, conveyance and delivery) and 1s. (collection and conveyance or conveyance and delivery). The scale of charges for sending parcels by rail depended on weight, 6d. being the lowest charge (for a parcel weighing not more than 3 lb.) increasing in 1d. stages to 9d. (for a parcel of 14 lb. or 15 lb.).

If the fares seem cheap, they should perhaps be compared with those charged on Green Line coach route D. This route, introduced on 4th October, 1933, ran direct from Westerham to Victoria, Eccleston Bridge, with a journey time of one hour 29 minutes. The single fare was 1s. 9d., the return 2s. 9d. The coach service was hourly and, although fairly slow, was clearly more attractive to any passengers who disliked 'dirty' steam trains and the thought of having to change at Dunton Green.

As for the purely local traffic, the bus had by the 1930s taken almost all of it away; who would choose to travel from Westerham to Sevenoaks by train, with an irritating change thrown in, when he or she could conveniently do the through trip by bus? Who in Brasted village would trek all the way up the lane to the station to take a train to Westerham or Chevening? In April 1914 East Surrey Traction Co. had inaugurated a bus route between Reigate, Oxted, Westerham, Brasted, Chipstead and Sevenoaks; it ran two-hourly, eight journeys each way and three on Sundays. Then in August 1921 it was supplemented by a new service S3, operating between West Croydon, Chelsham, Westerham, Brasted, Chipstead and Sevenoaks. The older route was numbered S24 in April 1922, by which time there were six buses a day each way on weekdays and five on Sundays; the journey time between Sevenoaks and

DUNTON GREEN, BRASTED, and WESTERHAM.

Down

Week Days — Morning — Afternoon

Miles from Dunton Green	Down				
	Charing Cross	dep.			
	Waterloo	"			
	Cannon Street	"			
	London Bridge	"			
	Dunton Green	dep.			
1¼	Chevening Halt	"			
3½	Brasted	"			
4½	Westerham	arr.			

NOTES

— SX Sats excepted
— S O Sats only

Down — Week Days—Cont.—Aft. / Sundays — Morning — Afternoon

W S O Weds and Sats only

WESTERHAM, BRASTED, and DUNTON GREEN

Up.

Week Days — Morning — Afternoon

Miles	Up.				
	Westerham	dep.			
1	Brasted	"			
3¼	Chevening Halt	"			
4½	Dunton Green	arr.			
23¾	London Bridge	arr.			
24	Cannon Street	"			
24¼	Waterloo	"			
25¼	Charing Cross	"			

NOTES

—
S O Sats only
S X Sats excepted

Up. — Aft.—Week Days—Cont. Aft. / Sundays — Morning — Afternoon

Timetable, 1938. From SR Suburban Passenger Timetable, 3rd July, 1938.

Westerham was 40 minutes [*Black's Guide to Kent*, 1923]. Route S3 became 403 in December 1924 and lasted for very many years, being taken over by the London Passenger Transport Board in July 1933; route S24, however, was withdrawn in June 1926, since when there was no direct route between Oxted and Sevenoaks until 27th May, 1995.

Another important bus route connected Westerham with Bromley. Communication between the two towns by rail was awkward, with changes at Dunton Green and Orpington, and so route S10 (Reigate, Oxted, Westerham, Biggin Hill, Bromley) when it began in June 1922 was very useful to the town's residents. However, it was not entirely competitive, as the S3 was, for in passing right by Westerham station it provided a useful feeder to the railway for short-distance travel, such as to Westerham Hill or to Limpsfield and Oxted in the opposite direction. The route was renumbered 410 in December 1924, passed to London Transport in July 1933 and, like the 403, lasted into recent times. In April 1922, East Surrey, in connection with the London General Omnibus Co., had opened a bus garage at Dunton Green, adjacent to the railway just west of the bridge carrying the Bromley to Sevenoaks road. The garage supplied buses for most of the routes running in the Sevenoaks area, although some of those used on route S10 were stabled overnight in the yard of the Crown Hotel, Westerham, until 1925.

Buses of the 1920s were open-topped, ran on solid tyres and were extremely slow. Covered-top buses, which had first made their appearance on the inner London routes in 1926, gradually came in on the country routes from about 1932, and being on pneumatic tyres were permitted to run at greater speeds. With the local traffic now carried by bus, almost the sole function of the railway was to convey season-ticket holders between its stations and London, plus a certain amount of long-distance traffic and a modicum of freight.

As an illustration of just how bus-minded the public had become by the late 1930s, the following recollection by R.W. Kidner is quoted below:

Westerham was always a favourite place for ramblers, being quite near London. I can recall around 1937 phoning Dunton Green garage for an extra bus one Sunday evening because the ramblers' group I was in could not get on to the bus because of the crowd in the square. I suppose rail was not considered as we were probably trying to get back to Bromley or Eltham.

One hopes that Dunton Green was able to whistle up a bus and crew at such short notice - it could never happen now!

In later years even Chevening Halt had its local traffic filched by newly introduced bus routes through the nearby village of Chipstead, which was served by the 454 and 413, direct to Sevenoaks. The Halt was used, however, by the seventh Earl Stanhope, of Chevening Park, two or three times a week when he needed to go to London; a great public figure, he was First Lord of the Admiralty during 1938/9 and Chairman of the trustees of the National Maritime Museum from 1934 to 1959.

Staff appointments and transfers were regularly recorded by the *Southern Railway Magazine*, the company's excellent house journal. Here are some of the staff changes in 1938 at Westerham:

May 1938	R.C. Mitchell, porter, to leading porter, Blackfriars
August 1938	H. Brown, porter, to relief porter, London East District
	G.S. Jordan, porter, from Dunton Green
September 1938	W. Penfold, signalman, retired
	H. Towner, porter-signalman, to signalman, Wateringbury
	G. New, porter from Dunton Green, to porter-signalman, Westerham
October 1938	A.E. Ivey, station lampman from Rotherhithe Road, to signalman, Westerham
	H.G. Smith, porter, from Dunton Green

Edward Ivey was to remain a signalman at Westerham for very many years and, on his retirement, continued to live in the town.

Up to the time of the declaration of war on Germany on 3rd September, 1939, the branch line carried on its duties quietly and unremarkably. The *Southern Railway Magazine* mentioned a 'slight mishap' that had occurred at Dunton Green on 23rd October, 1937, and reproduced a sketch drawn for the subsequent inquiry by porter-signalman A.G.F. Bridgland of the branch platform viewed from the western end. Brasted station was in the news in 1939 when it was unfortunate enough to receive the attention of a petty thief on the night of 25th July. Magistrates heard that, after going to the trouble of wrapping a brick in a handkerchief and hurling the missile through the booking office window, the miscreant had been content merely to walk off with two tickets (destination not stated) and a pair of pliers, valued at 7s. 5d.

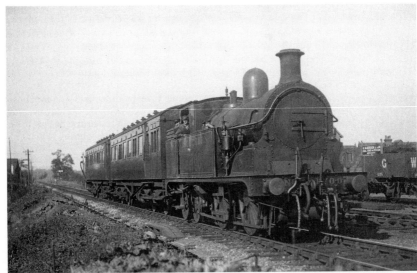

The typical branch train of the late 1930s: class 'R1' 0-4-4 tank locomotive No. 1700 with Set 481 or 482 enters Westerham station. In the goods yard were Great Western wagon No. 5179 and a board proclaiming 'G. Alderson & Son. Coal, Coke and Forage Merchants'.
Lens of Sutton

Chapter Seven

Southern Railway
1939 to 1947

From 1st September, 1939, all railways were put under government control. The Southern was required to evacuate many of London's children to country areas; over 7,000 evacuees arrived at Sevenoaks station in five days, but few if any used the Westerham branch as apparently buses were employed to distribute them to the surrounding villages, Sevenoaks being the 'railhead'. Local buses continued to run normal services but the Green Line coaches to London were discontinued as the vehicles had all been commandeered for ambulance work.

On the railways it was a time of great confusion. Cheap Day tickets were first withdrawn, then restored on 6th September. Then, from the 11th, drastically reduced train services were operated, details of which were posted at all stations. A week later came a decision to restore the normal 'Saturdays Excepted' schedules as from 18th September. Platform tickets were withdrawn, as were excursion and some other reduced-fare tickets, but not Monthly or Weekend Returns. Season and workmen's tickets were retained.

The travelling public had to suffer irksome 'black-out' regulations which were rigorously enforced. Main line trains after dark retained their lighting, but blinds had to be kept lowered and all windows shut during the journey. Local trains, such as those working the Westerham branch, were unable at first to have any lighting, owing to the frequent stops. On the stations, in an effort to prevent people from bumping into canopy-supports and other projections, or from falling off the platforms, white paint was daubed on the supports to give a chequered effect and the platform edges were white-lined. Windows were totally obscured and blue lamps were fitted at stations.

Expected air raids did not happen for several months, but during January 1940 branch line passengers did suffer from heavy snowfalls, which lasted some six weeks. Later in the year heavy bombing from the air every night was unrelenting, and on 12th October a high-explosive bomb fell on the line, 150 yards on the Dunton Green side of Chevening Halt, destroying the track. The branch had to be closed for six days, but at 4.30 pm on 18th October, 1940, the line was clear and train services restored.

Always seeking ways of cutting costs, the Southern in December 1939 drew up a plan to replace Westerham's signal cabin with a platform-level frame adjoining the booking office at the north-east end. There would have been 16 levers - including one spare - three more than in the existing cabin. Also proposed were a new up advanced starting upper-quadrant signal and some extra ground signals, including one to replace the SE&CR ringed signal that controlled the exit from No. 2 Siding. This plan does not show the westernmost connection between No. 1 and No. 2 Sidings, suggesting that either it had been abolished recently or was about to be. Estimated cost of all the signalling alterations was £720, but about mid-1940 the scheme was abandoned. Some other stations (such as Hever, Cowden, Ashurst and Martin Mill) were given signal frames adjoining their booking offices, thus enabling each of these stations to be run by one man,

'R1' No. 1710 and train at Westerham. Note that in this late-1930s view the connection between the run-round loop and the western end of the goods siding was still extant (*right foreground*).

Lens of Sutton

but perhaps the Southern decided that in Westerham's case the potential savings in operating costs were not great enough.

During the run of its series 'Through the Alphabet - London East Stations' the *Southern Railway Magazine*, in its July-August 1940 issue, took a look at the Westerham branch, giving brief descriptions of the villages that it passed near, the line itself and its peacetime traffic.

Westerham issued about 1,100 tickets a month, including 250 Cheap Day Returns to London. Each month about 100 Monthly Returns and 160 Weekend Returns were issued to passengers. Westerham was a favourite rail destination every weekend for large numbers of hikers, who would set forth to climb the nearby hills and penetrate neighbouring woodlands (and, in all probability, annoy the local landowners by dropping litter and failing to close gates!).

There was not much parcels traffic, but at frequent intervals heavy wireless apparatus, each package weighing 5½ cwt, was dispatched by passenger train to various parts of the country.

Brewing was noted as Westerham's chief industry, but there was no mention of any beer traffic on the railway; presumably by 1940 it was all going by road. In fact, goods traffic 'of a general character' was mainly incoming, general goods being approximately 3,000 tons annually. Minerals included 600 tons of incoming coal every month; and 300 tons per month of outgoing refuse and manure. There was also quite frequent traffic in containers, these being used chiefly for household furniture removals. Every autumn an appreciably large amount of beet-pulp was received at the branch-line terminus.

The timetable dated 5th May, 1941, shows that the full pre-war service was still operating, except that the late Wednesday train had been discontinued and on Sundays trains now ran only every two hours instead of hourly. There were 22 trains each way (Mondays to Fridays), 20 down and 21 up on Saturdays and eight down and seven up on Sundays. The weekday service began with the 6.16 am Westerham to Dunton Green, the stock having been berthed overnight, and after working the 8.38 am Westerham to Dunton Green the train ran to Tonbridge. The relieving set from Tonbridge took over with the 9.01 am Dunton Green to Westerham, returning to Tonbridge after the 12.19 pm (SO) or 1.54 pm (SX) Westerham to Dunton Green. On Mondays to Fridays the first set was back again on the branch, starting with the 2.25 pm Dunton Green to Westerham and finishing with the 11.30 pm Westerham to Dunton Green, whence it returned to Tonbridge. The second train also returned from Tonbridge, just to work the 6.03 pm Dunton Green to Westerham, where it was berthed for the 6.16 am next morning.

On Saturdays the first set returned from Tonbridge at noon to take over, starting with the 12.42 pm Dunton Green to Westerham and finishing with the 5.38 pm Westerham to Dunton Green where it was berthed for Sunday. The second train, which took over with the 6.00 pm to Westerham, had come up from Tonbridge to work the rest of the evening's services until the 11.30 pm Westerham to Dunton Green, whence it returned to Tonbridge.

On Sundays the train set that had been berthed at Dunton Green on Saturday worked all the branch trains, and finished its day at Westerham in order to work the first train thence on Monday morning.

To work the branch on Sundays during this period only one locomotive was required, an 'R1' class 0-4-4 tank engine, push-and-pull fitted, on Tonbridge Duty No. 303. From 11th October, 1942, it started work with the 6.05 am Tonbridge to Sevenoaks, ran light to Dunton Green, worked the branch starting with the 8.35 am Dunton Green to Westerham and finishing with the 9.35 pm Dunton Green to Westerham, ran light from Westerham to Sevenoaks and ended the duty with the 11.32 pm Sevenoaks to Tonbridge. As the coal supply could not have lasted all day there must have been coaling facilities at the site of Westerham's locomotive shed.

Three sets of men were needed to crew the locomotive, each of the duties being very far from arduous with only 22 minutes of actual driving every two hours! The first set of Tonbridge men worked during the morning until the 11.09 am Westerham to Dunton Green, and returned home 'passenger'. They were relieved at Dunton Green by Hither Green men, who arrived 'passenger' to work the 12.35 pm Dunton Green to Westerham and all trips until the 5.09 pm Westerham to Dunton Green, then returned home 'passenger'. The second set of Tonbridge men relieved the Hither Green crew at Dunton Green after having arrived there 'passenger' from their home depot, worked the 6.35 pm to Westerham and finished the duty at Tonbridge.

Since pleasure travel at this time was virtually non-existent, it is a matter for wonder that a Sunday service was retained at all, particularly when it had to be worked in such an expensive way. Probably there was a certain amount of Forces' leave traffic. The only thing that can be said is that wear-and-tear on the equipment was somewhat lessened by running trains every two hours instead of hourly, but it certainly was not a very productive use of engine crews.

By May 1944 two additional Sunday trains, the 7.57 am Dunton Green to Westerham and 8.17 am return, had been put on, and all up trains retimed to leave at 17 minutes past the odd hours. A change to the weekday carriage working had also occurred: the stock of the 6.03 pm (SX) Dunton Green to Westerham, instead of berthing there on arrival, formed the 7.23 pm up and worked the rest of the evening's train services, returning to Tonbridge after the 11.30 pm Westerham to Dunton Green. The other set, after working the 7.00 pm Dunton Green to Westerham, now berthed at Westerham overnight instead of continuing with the 7.23 pm up as formerly. In this way the two push-and-pull sets were rotated, the one starting at Tonbridge finishing at Westerham and vice versa. There was in addition a standby set berthed at Tonbridge. As before, one of the branch sets was berthed at Dunton Green between Saturday evening and Sunday morning.

From 6th October, 1941, first class facilities were withdrawn from the Westerham branch stations, as well as the electric local trains running on the Sevenoaks-London and other suburban services. This was to alleviate overcrowding, and the theory was that any train running wholly within the London Passenger Transport Board area was to have third class accommodation only. First class was in fact retained on steam trains, whether or not they ran wholly within the LT area, but push-and-pull sets Nos. 481/2 were formally downgraded to third class although not so-painted until 1951. Other push-and-pull sets retained their first class as they were needed for services outside the LT area, but whenever one of them showed up on the Westerham branch all their compartments were available to third class passengers, for there were no first class bookings from the branch stations.

Recorded wartime observations are few. On 8th April, 1944, Mr R.C. Riley noted former LB&SCR push-and-pull set No. 716 on the branch while he was passing through Dunton Green station; and a correspondent to the *Railway Observer* stated that on 18th November, 1944, class 'R1' No. 1700 was working the branch.

On 9th March, 1945, Mr J.H. Wildish, for many years the station master at Dunton Green and also responsible for all the branch stations, was presented with a cheque for £15 on his promotion as station master at Beckenham Junction and Kent House. The *SR Magazine* recorded that staff from Dunton Green, Brasted and Westerham attended the presentation, which was carried out by Mr Restall, Westerham's station clerk.

After 'VE' Day, 8th May, 1945, the Southern tried very hard to return to normal, but pre-war standards of cleanliness were almost impossible to attain. Branch line engines were grubby, stations were shabby, and the spectre of Nationalisation did much to discourage much in the way of effort; men and equipment were almost worn out after six years of operating in abnormal conditions. However, the branch train had no difficulty in maintaining connections at the junction, there were plenty of passengers, and the full hourly Sunday service was restored. There was now a great deal of freight traffic. A set of photographs taken in August 1947 shows that Westerham goods yard was full of wagons; there was still milk traffic in churns; and there was even a horsebox standing at the buffers at the end of the running road. The station building needed a repaint - which it did not get until about 1952 - and the canopy supports still bore their white 'black-out' stripes.

At some date between 1938 and 1947 the western crossover connecting the run-round loop to the goods-shed siding had been lifted, and a set of the necessary trap-points put into the run-round loop some yards west of where the 'Y' points had been. Presumably at the same time, the up main starting signal had been replaced by a standard SR upper-quadrant signal on a post made of two lengths of bullhead rail, bolted together. The up home signal also had a rail-built mast, but this signal was lower-quadrant. The SE&CR-type siding signal, with its black-ringed arm, remained in use.

Westerham goods yard even had its own mechanical horse by 1947. This was a very useful type of delivery lorry in which the driving portion, with three wheels, was articulated to the detachable trailer. Its registration number was DYH 642.

The station master at Dunton Green, Mr J.C. Saltmarsh, who had replaced Mr Wildish, did not stay long and, on 1st October, 1947, to mark his departure, he was presented with a table lamp and a cigarette lighter by F. Seal, on behalf of the staff of Dunton Green, Brasted and Westerham stations. His replacement was Mr E. Birch, transferred as station master from Etchingham.

Push-and-pull fitted locomotives allocated to Tonbridge in 1945-7 for working the Westerham branch and others were: class 'R' 0-4-4T Nos. 1670-72/75 and class 'R1' 0-4-4T Nos. 1700/03/04/07 - eight locomotives in all.

TONBRIDGE DUTY No. 310.

(R1 Class, P. & P. fitted.)

—	Tonbridge Loco.	3.30 a.m. ‖	A
4. 4 a.m.	Dunton Green	4.35 a.m.	F
	(2.20 a.m. ex Hither Gn. **M.X.**)		
	(3.29 a.m. ex Sevenoaks **M.O.**)		
4.55 a.m.	Westerham	5.25 a.m.	F
5.30 a.m.	Brasted	5.55 a.m.	F
6. 0 a.m.	Westerham	6.16 a.m.	P
6.27 a.m.	Dunton Green	6.34 a.m.	P
6.45 a.m.	Westerham	6.59 a.m.	P
7.10 a.m.	Dunton Green	7.26 a.m.	P
7.37 a.m.	Westerham	7.46 a.m.	P
7.57 a.m.	Dunton Green	8. 2 a.m.	P
8.13 a.m.	Westerham	8.38 a.m.	P
8.49 a.m.	Dunton Green	9.10 a.m.	E
9.14 a.m.	Sevenoaks	9.18 a.m.	E
9.26 a.m.	Otford	9.35 a.m.	P
9.42 a.m.	Sevenoaks	10.18 a.m.	P
10.32 a.m.	Tonbridge	** ‖	

SATURDAYS EXCEPTED.

—	Loco. Yard (Coal)	12. 0 p.m. ‖	
—	Tonbridge	12.10 p.m.	P
12.46 p.m.	Maidstone West	1. 4 p.m.	P
1.42 p.m.	Tonbridge	—	
—	Loco. Yard	5.15 p.m. ‖	
—	Tonbridge	5.45 p.m.	P
6. 3 p.m.	Edenbridge	6.10 p.m.	E
6.30 p.m.	Tonbridge	** ‖	
—	Loco. Yard	—	

TONBRIDGE DUTY No. 310—*continued.*

SATURDAYS ONLY.

—	Loco. Yard	11.35 a.m. ‖	
—	Tonbridge	11.59 a.m.	P
12.21 p.m.	Dunton Green ...	12.45 p.m.	P
12.56 p.m.	Westerham	1. 3 p.m.	P
1.14 p.m.	Dunton Green	1.20 p.m.	P
1.31 p.m.	Westerham	1.45 p.m.	P
1.56 p.m.	Dunton Green	2. 2 p.m.	P
2.13 p.m.	Westerham	2.23 p.m.	P
2.34 p.m.	Dunton Green	2.45 p.m.	P
2.56 p.m.	Westerham	3.40 p.m.	P
3.51 p.m.	Dunton Green	4. 0 p.m.	P
4.11 p.m.	Westerham	4.40 p.m.	P
4.51 p.m.	Dunton Green	5.10 p.m.	P
5.21 p.m.	Westerham	5.40 p.m.	P
5.51 p.m.	Dunton Green	** ‖	
—	Westerham	—	
	Shunting engine.		
	F—7.30 p.m.—9.0 p.m.		
—	Westerham	9.13 p.m.	F
9.38 p.m.	Dunton Green	** ‖	
—	Tonbridge Loco.	—	

Tonbridge Men.

1st set on duty 3.15 a.m.

2nd set (S.X.) off No. 304 duty, work 12.0 p.m. ‖ as shown.

S.O.—On duty 11.20 a.m., work as shown and home pass. from Dunton Green after relief

3rd set (S.X.) off No. 303 duty work 5.15 p.m. ‖ as shown and complete duty.

S.O.—Off No. 295 duty, relieve at Dunton Green and complete duty.

Engine Workings, from 16th June, 1947

TONBRIDGE DUTY No. 311.
(R.1 Class—P. & P. Fitted.)

—	Loco. Yard	... 5.45 a.m.	‖ A
5.50 a.m.	Tonbridge	... 6. 5 a.m.	P
6.21 a.m.	Sevenoaks	... 6.47 a.m.	P
7. 1 a.m.	Tonbridge	... 7.23 a.m.	P
7.43 a.m.	Dunton Green	... 9. 1 a.m.	P
9.12 a.m.	Westerham ...	... 9.16 a.m.	P
9.27 a.m.	Dunton Green	... 9.35 a.m.	P
9.46 a.m.	Westerham ...	... 9.54 a.m.	P
10. 5 a.m.	Dunton Green	...10.25 a.m.	P
10.36 a.m.	Westerham ...	...10.54 a.m.	P

SATURDAYS EXCEPTED.

11. 5 a.m.	Dunton Green	...11.25 a.m.	P
11.36 a.m.	Westerham ...	...11.54 a.m.	P
12. 5 p.m.	Dunton Green	...12.25 p.m.	P
12.36 p.m.	Westerham ...	...12.54 p.m.	P
1. 5 p.m.	Dunton Green	... 1.25 p.m.	P
1.36 p.m.	Westerham ...	... 1.54 p.m.	P
2. 5 p.m.	Dunton Green	... 2.12 p.m.	P
2.29 p.m.	Tonbridge	... ** p.m.	‖
—	Loco. Yard	... 4.45 p.m.	‖A
4.50 p.m.	Tonbridge	... 5. 0 p.m.	P
5.21 p.m.	Dunton Green	... 6. 3 p.m.	P
6.14 p.m.	Westerham ...	... 7.23 p.m.	P
7.34 p.m.	Dunton Green	... 7.40 p.m.	P
7.51 p.m.	Westerham ...	... 7.55 p.m.	P
8. 6 p.m.	Dunton Green	... 8.10 p.m.	P
8.21 p.m.	Westerham ...	... 8.40 p.m.	P
8.51 p.m.	Dunton Green	... 9. 0 p.m.	P
9.11 p.m.	Westerham ...	... 9.45 p.m.	P
9.56 p.m.	Dunton Green	...10.13 p.m.	P
10.24 p.m.	Westerham ...	...10.38 p.m.	P
10.49 p.m.	Dunton Green	...11. 0 p.m.	P
11.11 p.m.	Westerham ...	...11.30 p.m.	P
11.41 p.m.	Dunton Green	...11.57 p.m.	P
12.16 a.m.	Tonbridge	... **	‖
—	Loco. Yard	—	

[continued.

TONBRIDGE DUTY No. 311—*continued.*

SATURDAYS ONLY.

11. 5 a.m.	Dunton Green	...11.25 a.m.	P
11.36 a.m.	Westerham ...	...11.45 a.m.	P
11.56 a.m.	Dunton Green	...12. 0 noon	P
12.11 p.m.	Westerham ...	...12.19 p.m.	P
12.30 p.m.	Dunton Green	... 1.13 p.m.	P
1.29 p.m.	Tonbridge	... ** p.m.	‖
—	Loco. Yard	... 4.45 p.m.	‖A
—	Tonbridge	... 5. 5 p.m.	P
5.25 p.m.	Dunton Green	... 6. 0 p.m.	P
6.11 p.m.	Westerham ...	... 6.40 p.m.	P
6.51 p.m.	Dunton Green	... 7. 0 p.m.	P
7.11 p.m.	Westerham ...	... 7.40 p.m.	P
7.56 p.m.	Dunton Green	... 8. 0 p.m.	P
8.11 p.m.	Westerham ...	... 8.40 p.m.	P
8.51 p.m.	Dunton Green	... 9. 0 p.m.	P
9.11 p.m.	Westerham ...	... 9.45 p.m.	P
9.56 p.m.	Dunton Green	...10.13 p.m.	P
10.24 p.m.	Westerham ...	...10.40 p.m.	P
10.51 p.m.	Dunton Green	...11. 0 p.m.	P
11.11 p.m.	Westerham ...	...11.30 p.m.	P
11.41 p.m.	Dunton Green	...11.57 p.m.	P
12.16 a.m.	Tonbridge	... **	‖
—	Loco. Yard	—	

Tonbridge Men.

1st set on duty 5.30 a.m., relieved at Tonbridge 7.20 a.m., then work 7.45 a.m.‖ as shown for No. 309 duty.

2nd set on duty 7.0 a.m., relieve at Tonbridge 7.20 a.m. and work as shown.

3rd set on duty 4.30 p.m. and complete duty.

Class 'R1' 0-4-4 tank locomotive No. 1707 in grubby black propels its push-and-pull set (No. 481 or 482) into Chevening Halt while working a Westerham to Dunton Green service in September 1946.   *R.W. Kidner*

Class 'R' 0-4-4 tank locomotive No. 1671 of Tonbridge, with Set 717 standing-in for the normal branch train, at Westerham in August 1947, by which time the connection at the west end had been lifted. The Crown Hotel is visible, right background.

All had lost their handsome pre-war sage green livery and were in dirty black with a new style of shaded sans-serif lettering, the shading being malachite green. The intention was that most locomotives when they went through Works would emerge in malachite green livery, but Nationalisation occurred before this programme had progressed very far. The new masters were very keen on black, either lined-out or unlined, for all the smaller locomotives, with the result that wartime drabness was to be retained for many years after the war itself had ended.

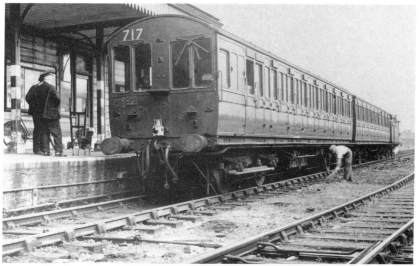

Two railwaymen and a dog ponder their next move at Westerham station, while Set 717 waits to be hauled to Dunton Green by class 'R' No. 1671. The trap points in the foreground have replaced the former connection between the loop and the siding.

Push-and-pull set No. 482 at Brasted, viewed from the field north-west of the station. Note G. Alderson & Son's board here, as at Westerham: 'Coal & Coke Merchants, Haulage Contractors', 3rd June, 1950.   *Denis Cullum*

Class 'H' No. 31523 worked the 11.45 am train out of Westerham on 19th April, 1952. Although it was fairly unusual for the engine to be at the Dunton Green end of the train, the presence of a parcels and miscellaneous van on the branch was even more so.   *James Aston*

Chapter Eight

British Railways, Southern Region

There was little change in the operation of the branch after state ownership of the railways was effected on 1st January, 1948. Class 'R' and 'R1' 0-4-4 tank locomotives from Tonbridge Shed continued working with push-and-pull sets 481/2 on all trains until about 1951; however, they were almost worn out and so gradually Wainwright's class 'H' 0-4-4 tank locomotives began to be fitted with the necessary control gear for working push-and-pull trains and many of these engines were transferred to Tonbridge. They began to take over the working of the branch in 1952 or earlier and soon it was rare to see an 'R' or 'R1' in use, although the last of them was not withdrawn until April 1956.

During the late 1940s Tonbridge still had a total of eight class 'R' and 'R1' locomotives at any one time for working the Westerham and other branches. The following engines were allocated between 1948 and 1956:

'R'	31665	May 51 to Sep. 52 ;	wdn
'R'	31666	May 51 to Dec. 55 ;	wdn
'R'	31667	Dec. 48 to May 51 ;	wdn
'R'	1670	to Apr. 51 ;	wdn (Renumbered 31670 Dec. 48)
'R'	1671	to Feb. 53 ;	transfd (Renumbered 31671 Nov. 49)
'R'	1672	to Dec. 49 ;	wdn
'R'	1675	to Oct. 52 ;	wdn
'R1'	1700	to Sep. 52 ;	wdn (Renumbered 31700 July 48)
'R1'	1703	to Feb. 54 ;	wdn (Renumbered 31703 July 50)
'R1'	1704	to Apr. 56 ;	wdn (Renumbered 31704 c. 48)
'R1'	31706	Oct. 50 to Nov. 52 ;	wdn
'R1'	1707	to Jan. 49 ;	wdn

The train service was disrupted for three weeks in 1948, from 29th February to 21st March, while the engineers had possession of Polhill tunnel on the main line and, except for 10 peak up trains each morning, no trains ran between Dunton Green and Knockholt. Special London Transport buses ran between these points, and a special train service ran on the branch to connect with these. A lorry conveyed parcels for Dunton Green and the branch. Westerham season-ticket holders were permitted to travel to London (Victoria) from Oxted.

With the start of the summer services on 31st May, 1948, the published engine workings were virtually the same as those for 1947. On weekdays three different engines were needed to work the line.

Duty No. 308
Saturdays Excepted. 1.05 pm Tonbridge to Dunton Green, 2.27 pm Dunton Green to Westerham and branch trips until 7.00 pm Dunton Green to Westerham; freight shunting at Westerham from 7.30 to 9.00 pm then 9.13 pm freight to Dunton Green; light to Tonbridge.

Duty No. 310

Light from Tonbridge, 3.40 am freight Sevenoaks to Dunton Green (Mondays Excepted), 4.35 am freight Dunton Green to Westerham, 5.25 am freight Westerham to Brasted and 5.55 am return, 6.16 am passenger Westerham to Dunton Green and branch trips until 8.38 am Westerham to Dunton Green, empty to Sevenoaks and 10.18 am Sevenoaks to Tonbridge.

Saturdays Only. 11.59 am Tonbridge to Dunton Green, 12.44 pm Dunton Green to Westerham and branch trips until 5.40 pm Westerham to Dunton Green. Light to Westerham, freight shunting 7.30 to 9.00 pm, 9.13 pm freight to Dunton Green, light to Tonbridge.

Duty No. 311

6.05 am Tonbridge to Sevenoaks and 6.47 am return; 7.23 am Tonbridge to Dunton Green, 9.01 am Dunton Green to Westerham and branch trips until:

Saturdays Excepted. 1.54 pm Westerham to Dunton Green, 2.12 pm Dunton Green to Tonbridge, 5.00 pm Tonbridge to Dunton Green, 6.03 pm Dunton Green to Westerham and branch trips until 11.30 pm Westerham to Dunton Green and 11.57 pm Dunton Green to Tonbridge.

Saturdays Only. 12.19 pm Westerham to Dunton Green, 1.13 pm Dunton Green to Tonbridge, 5.05 pm Tonbridge to Dunton Green, 6.00 pm Dunton Green to Westerham and branch trips until 11.30 pm Westerham to Dunton Green and 11.57 pm Dunton Green to Tonbridge.

From 23rd May, 1949, the 5.00 pm (SX) Tonbridge to Dunton Green was discontinued, being replaced by a 5.23 pm Tonbridge to Sevenoaks, worked by Duty 311. Continuing as empty stock to Dunton Green, this then formed the 6.23 pm to Westerham. The engine on Duty 308 now worked the 6.05 pm Dunton Green to Westerham instead of the 6.23; it then took over the 6.40 pm Westerham to Dunton Green and 7.02 pm return, then handed over the working of the 7.23 pm Westerham to Dunton to Duty 311. Other workings were the same as in 1948.

The next important change was the cessation on Saturdays of the 9.13 pm freight from Westerham to Dunton Green in 1951. Presumably the demand for freight movement on late Saturday evenings had declined to such an extent that it was no longer worth the trouble; the engine that formerly worked it now headed off light to Orpington after berthing at Dunton Green the stock of the 5.40 pm from Westerham, shunted at Orpington, then returned light to Tonbridge. On Mondays to Fridays the 9.13 pm freight was retimed to run at 11.20 pm from Westerham, as a mixed train attached to a push-and-pull set (empty), and the 11.30 pm passenger train was discontinued, except on Saturdays. On Saturdays the set berthed at Dunton Green to form the 7.55 am to Westerham on Sundays was now attached to the 11.57 pm Dunton Green to Tonbridge, presumably to enable a better rotation of the two sets each week.

Engine workings, on weekdays from 30th June, 1952, were now as under:

Duty No. 308 (booked for class 'R1')

Saturdays Excepted. 1.07 pm Tonbridge to Dunton Green, 2.25 pm Dunton Green to Westerham and branch trips until 6.40 pm Westerham to Dunton Green (double-headed with No. 311). Then light to Tonbridge.

Duty No. 310 (booked for class 'H' SX, class 'R1' SO)
    Light from Tonbridge, 3.40 am freight Sevenoaks to Dunton Green (Mondays Excepted), 4.35 am freight Dunton Green to Westerham, 5.25 am freight Westerham to Brasted and 5.55 am return, 6.16 am passenger Westerham to Dunton Green and branch trips until 8.38 am Westerham to Dunton Green, empty stock to Sevenoaks and 10.20 am Sevenoaks to Tonbridge.

Duty No. 311 (booked for class 'R1')
    6.05 am Tonbridge to Sevenoaks and 6.47 am return, 7.23 am Tonbridge to Dunton Green, 9.01 am Dunton Green to Westerham and branch trips until:
    Saturdays Excepted. 1.54 pm Westerham to Dunton Green, 2.12 pm Dunton Green to Tonbridge, 5. 23 pm Tonbridge to Sevenoaks, empty to Dunton Green, 6.23 pm Dunton Green to Westerham, 6.40 pm Westerham to Dunton Green (coupled to Duty 308), and branch trips until 9.00 pm Dunton Green to Westerham. Freight shunting 9.15 to 9.35 pm, then branch trips until 11.20 pm freight Westerham to Dunton Green, finishing with the 11. 57 pm passenger Dunton Green to Tonbridge.
    Saturdays Only. 12 .19 pm Westerham to Dunton Green, 1.13 pm Dunton Green to Tonbridge. 5. 05 pm Tonbridge to Dunton Green, 6.00 pm Dunton Green to Westerham and branch trips until 11.30 pm Westerham to Dunton Green and 11. 57 pm Dunton Green to Tonbridge (two push-and-pull sets) .

Duty No. 312 (booked for class 'R1')
    Saturdays Only. 11.59 am Tonbridge to Dunton Green, 12.44 pm Dunton Green to Westerham and branch trips until 5.40 pm Westerham to Dunton Green. Light to Orpington, freight shunting, light from Orpington to Tonbridge.

As stated earlier, a class 'H' was usually sent out by Tonbridge from 1952 and class 'R1' only rarely.

Since 1938, fares had risen by about two shillings, as the prices quoted in ABC Railway Guide for August 1949 show. There were no longer any Weekend Returns, and Day Returns were not available for return from London between 4.30 and 6.30 pm (Mondays to Fridays) or 12.00 noon and 1.30 pm (Saturdays). Many people still worked on Saturday mornings and lunchtime trains on that day were almost as busy as evening trains on other days.

	Ticket	Brasted 3rd	Westerham 3rd
Charing Cross	Single	4s. 11d.	5s. 2d.
Cannon Street	Single	4s. 8d.	4s. 11d.
London Bridge	Single	4s. 5d.	4s. 8d.
London	Monthly Return	7s. 0d.	7s. 0d.
London	Day Return	5s. 0d.	5s. 2d.

On 1st October, 1950, fares were revised, the charges being on a strict mileage basis within the London Transport area; at the same time return fares on Green Line coaches were abolished. In general, it meant that train fares were now slightly cheaper whilst bus fares were dearer - a 'levelling-up' exercise instigated by the British Transport Commission, the body set up by the Government to control all state-owned transport from 1948.

An unusual view showing the back of Westerham signal cabin, as the 6.18 pm train to Dunton Green leaves hauled by class 'H' No. 31548 on Duty No. 311, 21st May, 1955.   *R.C. Riley*

Class 'H' 0-4-4 tank locomotive No. 31544 with branch train at Dunton Green; this engine was allocated to Tonbridge between June 1954 and June 1956 only, thus dating the picture approximately.

Over the next few years it became clear that the service provided was somewhat lavish for the numbers of passengers presenting themselves and the method of working, requiring the use of several locomotives, several more sets of men, and two push-and-pull sets, was wasteful and loss-making, in terms of revenue. In 1955 the decision was made to restrict the service on Mondays to Fridays to mornings and early evenings only, on Saturdays to mornings and afternoons only (the last down train on weekdays leaving at 8.00 pm instead of 11.00 pm), and on Sundays to run an all-day service during spring, summer and autumn only. The hope was expressed that this economy would just enable the branch line to pay.

Until 1955 the branch was worked on the electric tablet system and the service was arranged to allow two trains on the line during the evening peak period. After the 6.05 pm from Dunton Green had arrived at Westerham and shunted to a siding to leave the platform clear, the 6.23 pm to Westerham was able to leave Dunton Green. There would then be two trains together at Westerham. All very slick, but with only minor adjustment it would have been possible to manage with just one push-and-pull set to work all services on the 'one engine in steam' principle - which was how the branch started life. And so, from the start of the winter timetable - 19th September, 1955 - the off-peak trains were withdrawn; sets 481/2 continued to be used, but only one at a time; only one engine was booked to work the Monday-to-Friday service, two on Saturdays and two on Sundays; and Sunday trains were suspended from 6th November, 1955, to 18th March, 1956. A miniature train staff was now under the control of the Dunton Green signalman. Brasted became an unstaffed halt, but Westerham itself retained its station staff and, moreover, continued to be fully signalled; so for a town whose population was still less than 4,000 the economies were not really very severe. The freight service too was retained and both Westerham and Brasted kept all their sidings.

British Railways, Southern Region, in the expectation that there would be howls of protest from passengers, issued a press release giving convincing reasons for the service reductions; and this was published in the *Sevenoaks News* for 15th September, 1955, under the authorship of F.D.Y. Faulkner, public relations and publicity officer at Waterloo:

Traffic on the Westerham Branch in the off-peak hours has been light for some time although an almost hourly service has been provided. This is understandable, as the rail route from Westerham to London and to Sevenoaks via Dunton Green is somewhat circuitous. There is a direct Green Line service to London via Westerham Hill and Bromley, and there are London Transport country bus services to Sevenoaks, Oxted, etc. The existing passenger services are unremunerative, even taking into account their contributory value to the main line.

Consequently we have had to seek means of achieving economy and starting with the winter timetable arrangements have been made to discontinue the off-peak weekday services (except on Saturdays when the service will continue from midday until about 8 pm) and to discontinue the Sunday service between 1st November and 24th March inclusive. The business trains, apart from comparatively slight adjustments, will remain unaltered.

By such means we will be able to operate the branch on a one engine in steam basis and achieve just enough economy to make the passenger service remunerative taking into account its contributory value to the main line.

Class 'H' No. 31164 and push-and-pull set No. 481 at Westerham, 29th April, 1956. On the right is the Crown, which, like the station, is no more. *Alan Snowdon*

The morning train for Dunton Green leaves Westerham on 29th April, 1956, with class 'H' No. 31164 and push-and-pull set No. 481; the houses in the background are in Madan Road. *Alan Snowdon*

We hope in this way to keep the line in being until such time as we can operate it by more modern and efficient methods of transport such as electrification or diesel-electrification, but I am bound to say that on account of its geographical position in relation to the main line railway routes Westerham will never be a very attractive passenger train service proposition except in the business periods when most of the present traffic is in fact carried.

Well worth noting is the fact that, despite what many recent writers have said, BR *was* aware of the value of contributory revenue of a branch line to a main line, even though the branch itself might have been losing money. Also noteworthy is that the Southern Region still had dreams of electrifying everything in sight, at a time when no progress in that direction was being made; diesel-electric trains, when they came in in 1957, never ran on the branch and even if they had they would not have saved it - they did not save any other similar short branch line. Finally it should be pointed out that Mr Faulkner, when mentioning the withdrawal of Sunday services, erred in his quoted dates, neither of which was a Sunday!

Had it not been for the healthy 'commuter' traffic the line might well have been closed there and then, but the authorities must have thought the branch deserved a chance. Many of the peak trains were filled to capacity with passengers travelling to and from London daily. Retention of the Sunday service was presumably considered worthwhile to encourage tourists: visitors to Quebec House perhaps, or ramblers exploring this area of great beauty would have been likely passengers on Sundays during the summer.

In 1956 the engine workings on weekdays were as shown below:

Duty No. 301 (class 'H')
Saturdays Only. 11.17 am empty stock Tonbridge to Dunton Green, 12.00 noon Dunton Green to Westerham and branch trips until 4.20 pm Westerham to Dunton Green, light to Tonbridge. One set of men throughout.

Duty No. 310 (class 'H')
5.00 am Tonbridge to Sevenoaks, light to Dunton Green, 5.35 am freight Dunton Green to Westerham, shunting 5.55 to 6 10 am. 6.16 am passenger Westerham to Dunton Green and branch trips until 9.54 am Westerham to Dunton Green, empty to Sevenoaks, 10.20 am Sevenoaks to Tonbridge.
Saturdays Excepted. 4.00 pm empty stock Tonbridge to Dunton Green, 4.25 pm Dunton Green to Westerham and branch trips until 8.00 pm Dunton Green to Westerham. Freight shunting 8.30 to 8.45 pm, then 8.50 pm freight Westerham to Dunton Green; freight shunting at Dunton Green, then light to Tonbridge.
Saturdays Only. Light from Tonbridge to Dunton Green, take over 5.00 pm Dunton Green to Westerham, branch trips until 8.00 pm Dunton Green to Westerham, empty to Dunton Green, berth stock then light to Tonbridge. Worked by one set of men in the morning and another set in the afternoon.

SUNDAYS Until 28th October and again beginning 24th March, 1957:

Duty No. 302 (class 'H')
6.45 am Tonbridge to Sevenoaks, light to Dunton Green, 7.55 am Dunton Green to Westerham and branch trips until 12.28 pm Westerham to Dunton Green. Light to Tonbridge. One set of men throughout.

Duty No. 303 (class 'H')
Light engine Tonbridge to Dunton Green, take over 12.55 pm Dunton Green to Westerham and all branch trips until 10.00 pm Dunton Green to Westerham. Berth stock, then light to Sevenoaks; 11.32 pm Sevenoaks to Tonbridge. Two sets of men: first set relieved at Dunton Green 5.40 pm home passenger; second set passenger from Tonbridge, relieve at Dunton Green 5.40 pm.

Incidentally, because the 6.45 am Tonbridge to Sevenoaks and 11.32 pm return were trains that ran all year round, they had to be worked by other duties during the winter, necessitating more light-engine mileage. The suspension of Sunday services on the branch obviated the steaming of just one tank locomotive and the use of two sets of men; not a great saving really.

As for the push-and-pull set in use, this continued to be berthed overnight at Westerham, except on Saturday nights when it was left at Dunton Green. During the midday berthing at Tonbridge on weekdays it was possible to exchange sets if necessary.

On weekday mornings there were seven up trains and five down (plus one empty). The afternoon service comprised seven down and six up, Mondays to Fridays, and 10 down and nine up, plus one empty, on Saturdays. On Sundays there were 15 down and 14 up trains.

During the busiest part of the peak-hour service it proved possible to run trains at 30-minute intervals; in order to do this some of the turn-rounds were as tight as three minutes. Later, part of the Saturday lunchtime service was similarly improved to half-hourly; it all worked well as long as the railwaymen still abided by the maxim of Sidney Smart, the superintendent of operation: 'Punctuality is *really* necessary.'

Some time during the 1950s, certainly by 1952, the bridge over the line at Chevening Halt was reconstructed and the old sleeper-built platform was replaced by one made up from standard slabs of ferro-concrete in the approved Southern Railway/Region style. Other than that, the appearance of the line under British Railways' ownership changed but little. The station buildings took on a neglected air, even by 1957 when, although clearly due for repainting, nothing was done.

On four Sundays in September 1956 - 9th, 16th, 23rd and 30th - the main line was blocked at Sevenoaks station while work was carried out there. On the Saturdays the class 'H' locomotive and its push-and-pull set, after working the last train from Westerham to Dunton Green, continued empty to Rotherhithe Road; then, on the Sunday mornings it worked a special passenger train from London Bridge to Sevenoaks via Swanley to cover for the diverted 4.05 am London Bridge to Hastings. The train then worked empty to Dunton Green in time to take up its first branch working, the 7.55 am to Westerham.

Tuesday 15th January, 1957, saw what the *Railway Observer* described as the first special train to run on the branch for many years. The empty stock to form this special ran from Dunton Green to Westerham with class 'D1' No. 31487 (Tonbridge) at the front and class 'West Country' No. 34017 *Ilfracombe* (Stewarts Lane) at the rear of the 11-coach train of Maunsell corridor stock. The train left Westerham at 12.15 pm headed by the 'West Country' and propelled by the class 'D1', which presumably came off at Dunton Green; the destination of this children's excursion was Kensington Olympia. The return train in the evening was unable to run through to Westerham as the branch train was now running and so the special had to terminate at Dunton Green. Although the *Railway Observer* (February 1957) stated that the branch train was strengthened to take the Westerham parties, it does not say how; presumably a second push-and-pull set was brought up from Tonbridge and the class 'H' worked the two as a 'sandwich' formation.

Special instructions were issued for working trains with an engine at each end, as under:

> TRAINS WORKING WITH ENGINE AT EACH END. - Loaded and empty passenger trains, as advised by the Line Traffic Manager, may work with an engine at each end between Dunton Green and Westerham.
>
> The rear engine must be coupled to the train and the continuous brake must be effective throughout. Before starting, the guard must remind the driver of the train engine that an engine is attached to the rear of the train.
>
> The driver and fireman of the train engine will be responsible for the observance of signals and the working of the continuous brake. The driver of the engine in the rear must watch for and act upon signals given by the driver of the train engine, but is not relieved from the due observance of all signals affecting the working of the train.

The branch saw yet another special in 1957, this time on Sunday, 10th November, this being the 'Kentish Heights' ramblers' excursion from Greenford, Western Region. A cleaned class 'O1', No. 31064 of Stewarts Lane, took over the eight-coach train of WR corridors at Kensington from the recently-restored museum piece, *City of Truro*, and worked the excursion through to Westerham via Balham, Crystal Palace and Beckenham Junction. The 'O1' also worked the train back from Westerham to Kensington, this time via the Birkbeck spur, Norwood Junction and Selhurst; the *Railway Observer* for December 1957 reported that time was lost in both directions. Incidentally, although the GWR 4-4-0 *City of Truro* was effectively barred from the Southern Region because of its width, it was permitted to work just one special train, as far as East Croydon, on 11th May, 1958.

From time to time the branch was affected by extreme weather conditions: *Kent Weather Book* noted that on 31st March, 1952 the area received heavy snow, but the worst happening was a great rainstorm on Friday 5th September, 1958, over the whole South-East. The branch was cut off; there was an earthslip between Dunton Green and Chevening, and the embankment was breached near Madan Road. In the town itself Quebec House was damaged by floodwater. Flooding blocked Sevenoaks tunnel and main line trains had to run via Oxted or Redhill for three days. Branch train services were unable to be restored until later the following week, when the line was reopened. Push-and-pull set 482 had been isolated at Westerham for the whole period.

Until 1959 the two ex-railmotor push-and-pull sets, Nos. 481/2, continued to be the line's special preserve, with a guard or junior porter selling Bell-Punch-type tickets from a wooden rack. Regular passengers were used to the fact that the carriage doors opened inwards but strangers, apparently, could not cope; according to Ivan P. Russell, in *Bluebell News* May 1961, more than one stranger 'tried to gain admittance by banging at the seemingly obstinate portal'.

When necessary the locomotive, with its carriages, would shunt to the Westerham water column between arrival and departure of the scheduled passenger trains and refill its tanks. Thus it was that in 1959 the 9-year-old Tom Burnham was able to secure this unusual shot. The column had been strengthened with a length of bullhead rail because of damage at an earlier date.

After 53 years' life, in one form or another, these sets were at last withdrawn, No. 481 at the end of 1959 and No. 482 early in 1960. For a time during 1960 ex-London, Brighton & South Coast Railway gangwayed push-and-pull sets appeared on the line (which they had on occasion done before), No. 723 being employed until its withdrawal in September 1960. There were also, during 1960, appearances of push-and-pull sets made up in 1943 from London & South Western corridor coaches; No. 732 (withdrawn in December 1960) and probably No. 735, the last survivor of this series, withdrawn in February 1961.

In 1959 the Southern Region conceived a most luxurious type of push-and-pull set. One coach was an SR open Second with drop windows, built in 1930; the gangway at the locomotive end was removed and the hole sheeted over, and the lavatory compartments were closed off. The other coach was a 1935-built SR corridor Brake Composite with two first-class and four second-class compartments; part of the luggage area was taken over for the driving controls, the gangway removed and the hole sheeted over, with two small windows added. The side duckets were replaced by sliding windows. Twenty of these sets were knocked up, numbered 600-19, and from about July 1960 three, Nos. 609, 610 and 611, were allocated to the Tonbridge area for Westerham and Hawkhurst branch working. Rather belatedly, passengers could now enjoy the comforts of Maunsell corridor stock, which was wider than the old railmotor sets; total seating capacity in each set was 100, including the first class - as there were no first class bookings on the branch the compartments were available to all. Westerham's regular set during 1961 was No. 610. Whilst there may have been a little variety in carriage stock provision during these years, nothing better than the reliable and long-lasting class 'H' was ever found. A very large number of these engines was allocated to Tonbridge during the 1950s and early 1960s (not all at the same time) and any one of these push-and-pull fitted machines could have worked, and in most cases did work, the branch. What is believed to be the complete roster is shown below. Many of them, on being transferred to Tonbridge, had only recently been fitted with air-control gear.

	Push-and-Pull Fitted	At Tonbridge
1164	July 49	Sep 49 to Nov. 50, Oct. 51 to Oct. 59; wdn
31177	May 53	Mar. 51 to Aug. 61; wdn
31184	June 52	May 51 to Mar. 58; wdn
31193	Sep. 52	May 48 to Apr. 61; wdn
31239	July 52	May 51 to Jan. 60; wdn
31263	Feb. 60	Apr. 60 to Oct. 61; transfd
31266	Apr. 58	May 58 to Sep. 60; wdn
31279	Feb. 53	June 58 to Sep. 59; wdn
31295	Apr. 52	June 58 to May 59; wdn
31308	Dec. 53	Feb. 61 to Oct. 61; transfd
31319	July 50	- 59 to Jan. 60; wdn
31322	Feb. 50	Feb. 61 to Apr. 61; wdn
31324	Jan. 61	Feb. 61 to Oct. 61; transfd
31500	Nov. 59	Nov. 59 to June 61; wdn
31512	Nov. 51	May 59? to June 61; wdn
31517	Dec. 49	Jan. 50 to Oct. 51, June 55 to June 61; wdn
31518	Mar. 52	May 59? to Oct. 61; transfd

On 7th May, 1960, the branch locomotive again takes water at Westerham. Visible here are the brick base of the former engine shed, the SE&CR goods signal and, to illustrate the free-and-easy atmosphere, two unauthorised boys by the track. Madan Road residents often used this as a short cut. *James Aston*

The 9.52 am train for Dunton Green leaves Westerham, with class 'H' No. 31553 and push-and-pull set No. 723 (which had replaced the withdrawn ex-SE&CR sets), 7th May, 1960. *James Aston*

	Push-and-Pull Fitted	At Tonbridge
31519	July 52	- 60 to Feb. 61; wdn
31520	June 49	July 49 to Mar. 50, - 59 to Aug. 60; wdn
31523	July 49	Sep. 49 to Jan. 59 ; wdn
31530	June 53	July 53 to June 56, Mar. 61 to Oct. 61; wdn Feb. 62
31533	c. 60	May 60 to June 61; transfd
31543	Oct. 53	Nov. 53 to c. 59; Oct. 60 to June 61; transfd
31544	June 54	June 54 to June 56; transfd
31548	Nov. 49	Jan. 50 to May 58; transfd
31551	Sep. 60	Oct. 60 to June 61; transfd
31553	Jan. 60	Feb. 60 to June 61; transfd
31554	Apr. 52	Jun. 52 to Apr. 57; transfd

In March 1960 two class 'M7' 0-4-4 tank locomotives appeared at Tonbridge Shed and in mid-March one of them, No. 30379, was recorded as working the branch: they were transferred away in August.

The 1960 timetable still showed seven up and five down trains, plus one down empty, on weekday mornings; seven down and six up afternoon trains on Mondays to Fridays, and 10 down and nine up on Saturday afternoons - plus one empty to berth at Dunton Green for the first down train on Sundays during the summer season. On Sundays between 20th March and 23rd October the full service of 15 down and 14 up trains was still maintained; it restarted on 19th March, 1961, and ceased after 22nd October, 1961.

By 1960, even the economy train service being operated was reckoned as not paying, and so British Railways initiated closure procedures. Southern Region informed the South Eastern Transport Users' Consultative Committee (TUCC) in spring 1960 that it wished to close the branch completely and estimated that closure would, even after allowing for the cost of providing extra bus services in replacement, save £11,600 a year. Compared with the losses of £25,500 per annum incurred on the Allhallows branch, which was put up for closure to passengers at the same time, the deficit looked quite small, and if the 'basic railway' - which was little more than a siding upon which a diesel railcar shuttled up and down - had been conceived in 1960 instead of 1964 the branch could well have been retained. It may well be that the losses were not even as great as those officially quoted; it was customary for contributory revenue to be omitted from the calculations and there was a suspicion that the costs of running empty trains between Tonbridge and Dunton Green were all charged to the deficit. No one knew, or was expected to question, how BR arrived at its figures, which had more than a suggestion of emanating from Keith Waterhouse's fictitious 'Department of Guesswork'.

The *Railway Magazine*, which was seldom critical of BR, remarked in its May 1960 issue that 'traffic is very light', presumably to justify the closure proposal; but there were about 200 regular passengers each day who would suffer considerable hardship if the branch closed.

And it was possible hardship to passengers that the Transport Users' Consultative Committees, originally set up under the 1947 Transport Act, were intended to take into consideration whenever a railway was proposed for closure. So far, they had not been very effective, and branches had been closed

The 1.20 pm train from Dunton Green arrives at Westerham with the same engine and carriages, 7th May, 1960. One passenger awaits the train, and in the goods yard there are only a couple of wagons.   *James Aston*

Class 'H' No. 31553 propels the 2.23 pm from Westerham through Park Wood, between Westerham and Brasted, on 7th May, 1960.   *James Aston*

all over the country without much resistance. Towards the end of 1960 the London Area TUCC announced that it had no objection to the Southern Region's proposal to close the branch; but in May 1961 the Central Transport Users' Consultative Committee recommended that the branch stay open as a social necessity.

It is doubtful whether there was dancing in the streets when this news was received, but most people believed that the line was saved and that BR had been compelled to continue running the train service. 'The first commuters' branch line that British Railways have ever attempted to close,' wrote one correspondent (Peter T. Winham) to the *Railway Modeller* in June. 'I would add that they were unsuccessful.'

But he (and many others) had reckoned without the Minister of Transport, Ernest Marples, who in August 1961 took the undemocratic step of rejecting the TUCC's recommendation that the line stay open, and decreed that it must close. The chairman of what was described by the *Sevenoaks News* (10th August, 1961) as the Passenger Users' Association, Hugh Farmer, commented: 'This is, I believe, the first time the Minister has gone directly against a recommendation of the Committee. The announcement made by a written Parliamentary reply just before the House rises gives us little opportunity for further protest.'

No doubt that was the general idea . . .

The correspondence columns of the local press buzzed. One writer felt that if the branch could be run by an independent company, with all its rolling stock and its few employees based locally, overheads and staff costs would be much less than with BR, still using expensive steam locomotives based at Tonbridge. He believed that an old motor coach fitted with flanged wheels would be just the thing for Westerham, and its maintenance could be undertaken by local garagemen as part of their normal work; its driver could also sell tickets and might possibly be a retired BR driver.

Two weeks later the line traffic manager of the South Eastern Division, T.R.V. Bolland, announced the closure date as Monday 30th October, 1961, although as by then there would be no Sunday service the last trains would run on Saturday the 28th. The 180 season-ticket holders were to be permitted to use the Westerham-Sevenoaks bus, changing at Sevenoaks to or from the London trains.

The editor of *Trains Illustrated*, Geoffrey Freeman Allen, took a dim view of the proceedings. 'The Minister of Transport is responsible to the public, but in arbitrarily setting aside the Central Committee recommendations on the branch he has cut across a procedure of democratic government,' he thundered in the October 1961 issue. It was now clear that submissions to TUCCs and a public inquiry were a 'time-wasting nonsense' as the Minister could always intervene to overturn a recommendation.

The *Railway Magazine*, in contrast, contented itself with the observation: 'Had the junction with the main line been made at Sevenoaks, and not at Dunton Green, the position today might be very different.'

Closure notices were posted at the stations concerned, warning of the cessation of both passenger and freight services, but promising that 'British Railways will continue to provide collection and delivery services for parcels and freight sundries traffic throughout the area and facilities for truck load

Saturday engine changeover at Dunton Green, 14th May, 1960. Class 'H' No. 31520 on Duty No. 303 is on the 12.50 pm to Westerham, and sister engine No. 31500 on Duty No. 306 waits to take over the 1.20 pm and work the rest of the afternoon service.   *James Aston*

The 4.50 pm Dunton Green to Westerham at Brasted, with class 'H' No. 31500, on 14th May, 1960. Changes since 1933 were few and the station, although unstaffed, still looked quite presentable.   *James Aston*

traffic exist at other stations in the vicinity.' Further information was available from Sevenoaks and Dunton Green stations, or the line traffic manager of the South Eastern Division, whilst for details of bus services in the area people were advised to seek information from No. 55 Broadway, London, or from 'any local office'. At Chevening Halt this notice was posted adjacent to one advertising Shopping Tickets to London, which, costing 4s. 9d., were available on Wednesdays and Thursdays only by any train after 9.30 am for return from London by 4.30 pm. One wonders how many shoppers took advantage of this 'offer' in the few weeks remaining to them. The single fare from Westerham to Dunton Green at this time was 1s. 1d.

In October a petition was signed by nearly 2,500 local people, and hundreds of letters were received by the Member of Parliament for Sevenoaks, John Rodgers, who forwarded them to Mr Marples. Mr Rodgers duly presented the petition in the House asking Mr Marples to rescind his decision. On 19th October he was informed by the Minister that the train service showed a loss of £26,000 per annum: over £150 for every regular passenger.

Mr Marples continued:

> It is an enormous loss. When we look at it in perspective, it is terrific. After very careful consideration, I myself have taken the decision. I have gone to look at the line and to walk in the area on weekdays and Sundays. I used dark glasses so that no one would recognise me, because I felt I might hear some of the things I have been reading in letters from my constituents, and I did not want to be subject to that indignity. I take full responsibility for my decision . . . constituents must not blame anybody else.

In just one year, apparently, the loss on working the line had more than doubled, although it seems unbelievable that such a short line, with only a modest train service, could possibly lose so much. *Trains Illustrated* considered that the branch train was inexpensive to run, and the locomotive could be used in the middle of the day for other services. But it also thought that a diesel multiple unit would be unsuitable for the line as it could not be sufficiently utilised.

The ' Flyer', as the branch train had become known, even achieved national fame in its last days: it was written-up in *The Times* for 11th August, 1961. After giving a brief history of the line, the writer described the carriages currently employed:

> The two in use now for the 11-minute trip still carry the Southern Railway monogram within. One is a compartmented, corridor coach - necessary, since the guard both collects and issues tickets in addition to performing his other duties. The other has a central gangway, and what can only be described as an entrance hall, complete with coconut doormats. An exhortation to 'Travel by Golden Arrow' seems somehow anachronistic. Apter in the context is a framed reproduction of a Kentish oast house, which has been upside down for as long as anyone can remember.

The suggestion was made that the real reason for hastening the line's end was that the land was required for the construction of a South Orbital road; and there was even a suspicion that Mr Marples personally wanted the line closed because he was not unconnected with the road-building firm of Marples,

C332 WEEKDAYS — WESTERHAM BRANCH

(Time allowance at Chevening Halt and Brasted Halt is 15 seconds unless otherwise shown)

DOWN

M. C.			Rail Motor	Rail Motor		ECS Rail Motor	Rail Motor		Rail Motor	Rail Motor						
			am	am		am	am		am	am						
0 00	**DUNTON GREEN** Ⓣ dep	1	6 34	7 23	..	7†54	8 26	..	9 6	9 37	..	..	..	..	..	..
1 24	Chevening Halt	2	6 36½	7 25½	......	......	8 28½	......	9 8½	9 39½	......	......	......	......	......	......
3 06	Brasted Halt	3	6 41½	7 30½	..	..	8 33½	..	9 13½	9 44½	..	..	..	..	..	..
4 56	**WESTERHAM** .... Ⓣ arr	4	6 45	7 34	......	8† 3	8 37	......	9 17	9 48	......	......	......	......	......	......

MONDAYS TO FRIDAYS

						Rail Motor	Rail Motor	Rail Motor	Rail Motor	Rail Motor	Rail Motor		Rail Motor			
						PM	PM	PM	PM	PM	PM		PM			
DUNTON GREEN .. dep	1	..	..	..	..	4 20	4 56	5 26	6 7	6 32	7 5	..	7 50	..	..	..
Chevening Halt	2	......	......	......	......	4 22½	4 58½	5 28½	6 9½	6 34½	7 7½	......	7 52½	......	......	......
Brasted Halt	3	..	..	..	..	4 27½	5 3½	5 33½	6 14½	6 39½	7 12½	..	7 57½	..	..	..
WESTERHAM ...... arr	4	......	......	......	......	4 31	5 7	5 37	6 18	6 43	7 16	......	8 1	......	......	......

SATURDAYS

		Rail Motor	Rail Motor	Rail Motor		Rail Motor	Rail Motor	Rail Motor	Rail Motor	Rail Motor	Rail Motor		Rail Motor			
		am	PM	PM		PM	PM	PM	PM	PM	PM		PM			
DUNTON GREEN .. dep	1	11 50	12 50	1 20	..	1 50	2 50	3 50	4 50	5 50	6 50	..	7 50	..	..	..
Chevening Halt	2	11 52½	12 52½	1 22½	......	1 52½	2 52½	3 52½	4 52½	5 52½	6 52½	......	7 52½	......	......	......
Brasted Halt	3	11 57½	12 57½	1 27½	..	1 57½	2 57½	3 57½	4 57½	5 57½	6 57½	..	7 57½	..	..	..
WESTERHAM ...... arr	4	12 1	1 1	1 31	......	2 1	3 1	4 1	5 1	6 1	7 1	......	8 1	......	......	......

SUNDAYS

Until 22nd October inclusive and again commencing 18th March 1962.

		Rail Motor	Rail Motor	Rail Motor	Rail Motor	Rail Motor	Rail Motor	Rail Motor	Rail Motor	Rail Motor	Rail Motor	Rail Motor	Rail Motor	Rail Motor	Rail Motor	Rail Motor
		am	am	am	am	am	PM	PM	PM	PM	PM	PM	PM	PM	PM	PM
DUNTON GREEN .. dep	1	7 50	8 50	9 50	10 50	11 50	12 50	1 50	2 50	3 50	4 50	5 50	6 50	7 50	8 50	9 50
Chevening Halt	2	7 52½	8 52½	9 52½	10 52½	11 52½	12 52½	1 52½	2 52½	3 52½	4 52½	5 52½	6 52½	7 52½	8 52½	9 52½
Brasted Halt	3	7 57½	8 57½	9 57½	10 57½	11 57½	12 57½	1 57½	2 57½	3 57½	4 57½	5 57½	6 57½	7 57½	8 57½	9 57½
WESTERHAM .. .. arr	4	8 1	9 1	10 1	11 1	12 1	1 1	2 1	3 1	4 1	5 1	6 1	7 1	8 1	9 1	10 1

The final Working Timetable, from 12th June, 1961 - Down Trains

(Time allowance at Chevening Halt and Brasted Halt is 15 seconds unless otherwise shown)

UP

M.C.		No	Rail Motor	Rail Motor		Rail Motor	Rail Motor	Rail Motor	Rail Motor		Rail Motor
			am	am		am	am	am	am		am
0 00	WESTERHAM .. Ⓣ dep	1	6 10	6 59	..	7 38	8 10	8 40	9 21	..	9 52
1 50	Brasted Halt	2	6 13½	7 2½		7 41½	8 13½	8 43½	9 24½		9 55½
3 32	Chevening Halt	3	6 18	7 7		7 46	8 18	8 48	9 29		10 0
4 56	DUNTON GREEN Ⓣ arr	4	6 21	7 10		7 49	8 21	8 51	9 32		10 3

MONDAYS TO FRIDAYS

	No	Rail Motor	Rail Motor		Rail Motor	Rail Motor	Rail Motor	Rail Motor
		PM	PM		PM	PM	PM	PM
WESTERHAM .. .. dep	1	4 42	5 12	..	5 49	6 21	6 47	7 23
Brasted Halt	2	4 45½	5 15½		5 52½		6 50½	7 26½
Chevening Halt	3	4 50	5 20		5 57		6 55	7 31
DUNTON GREEN.. arr	4	4 53	5 23		6 0	6 29	6 58	7 34

SATURDAYS

	No	Rail Motor	Rail Motor	Rail Motor	Rail Motor	Rail Motor	Rail Motor		Rail Motor	Rail Motor	Rail Motor	ECS Rail Motor
												*
		PM	PM	PM	PM	PM	PM		PM	PM	PM	PM
WESTERHAM .. .. dep	1	12 23	1 5	1 35	2 23	3 23	4 23	..	5 23	6 23	7 23	8†10
Brasted Halt	2	12 26½	1 8½	1 38½	2 26½	3 26½	4 26½		5 26½	6 26½	7 26½	
Chevening Halt	3	12 31	1 13	1 43	2 31	3 31	4 31		5 31	6 31	7 31	
DUNTON GREEN.. arr	4	12 34	1 16	1 46	2 34	3 34	4 34		5 34	6 34	7 34	8†19

* Until 21st October inclusive and again commencing 17th March 1962.

SUNDAYS

Until 22nd October inclusive and again commencing 18th March 1962.

	No	Rail Motor	Rail Motor	Rail Motor	Rail Motor	Rail Motor	Rail Motor	Rail Motor		Rail Motor	Rail Motor	Rail Motor	Rail Motor	Rail Motor	Rail Motor	Rail Motor
		am	am	am	am	PM	PM	PM		PM	PM	PM	PM	PM	PM	PM
WESTERHAM ...... dep	1	8 23	9 23	10 23	11 23	12 23	1 23	2 23	..	3 23	4 23	5 23	6 23	7 23	8 23	9 23
Brasted Halt	2	8 26½	9 26½	10 26½	11 26½	12 26½	1 26½	2 26½		3 26½	4 26½	5 26½	6 26½	7 26½	8 26½	9 26½
Chevening Halt	3	8 31	9 31	10 31	11 31	12 31	1 31	2 31	..	3 31	4 31	5 31	6 31	7 31	8 31	9 31
DUNTON GREEN.. arr	4	8 34	9 34	10 34	11 34	12 34	1 34	2 34		3 34	4 34	5 34	6 34	7 34	8 34	9 34

The final Working Timetable, from 12th June, 1961 - Up Trains

Class 'D1' 4-4-0 locomotive No. 31739 of Bricklayers Arms with special 7-coach train at Dunton Green (Set No. 277) on the last day of operation of the Westerham branch, 28th October, 1961.

Last day of train services on the Westerham branch, 28th October, 1961. Class 'D1' 4-4-0 No. 31739 comes off the train, presumably to take water. Note the top-hatted 'mourner' on the right.

Ridgway. When John Rodgers relayed his constituents' allegations, he received a written reply from the Parliamentary Secretary at the Minister of Transport which, in the light of subsequent events, is noteworthy:

> When we had our talk on 13th September about the closure of the Westerham-Dunton Green line you mentioned to me a current rumour that the Minister might have been influenced in reaching his decision by the possibility that certain proposed road improvements could be more economically carried out if the line were closed. I have made careful enquiries and I can assure you that any such suggestion is unfounded . . . The line of the road has not yet been fixed, and the Minister has not yet authorised any detail survey.

It is of interest that one of the officials at the Ministry of Transport at this time, and one moreover who was a user of the line, was Sir David Serpell, the deputy permanent secretary, later to achieve fame as the author of a report that proposed a very large number of railway closures. Shortly after the first edition of this book was published I received a letter from him, in which he stated: 'I used the line for a good many years (for some of them walking daily to Brasted station from halfway-up Brasted Chart) and was involved, as an official at the Ministry of Transport, with those difficult closure discussions.' He did not consider that the closure decision was in any way high-handed.

And so the battle to retain the line was lost, and the closure date, Saturday 28th October, arrived. It was a day of glorious autumn sunshine, and photographers were well in evidence. Morning and lunchtime trains were worked by class 'H' 0-4-4 tank locomotive No. 31518 on Tonbridge Duty No. 239, with the usual two-coach push-and-pull set. Shortly after noon at Westerham the front of the locomotive was adorned with a Union Flag and the inscription 'Flyer 1881-1961' was chalked on the smokebox. This train worked until the 2.23 pm to Dunton Green, where it was replaced by a seven-coach corridor set of BR standard stock, No. 277, which had worked empty from Rotherhithe Road carriage sidings. This set , with class 'D1' 4-4-0 No. 31739 of Bricklayers Arms at the western end and class 'Q1' 0-6-0 No. 33029 of Tonbridge at the eastern end, worked all the services starting with the 2.50 pm Dunton Green to Westerham. This was necessary to accommodate all the passengers who had come to ride on the line, including photographers, tape-recordists and even 'enthusiasts', one of whom said he travelled on branch lines only on their last day of operation.

The last scheduled train was the 7.50 pm Dunton Green to Westerham. At Westerham squibs and bangers were ignited. Octogenarian Mrs Jane Graves, who had been a passenger on the first train in 1881 and was on the last one that evening, was presented with a bouquet from members of her family. She shook hands with the driver of No. 33029, Mr Alfred Gilan, and informed the Press that her brother, Major A. Waters, had registered his protest at the closure from Bangalore!

The writer of the report ('Last Journey of the Flyer') that appeared in the *Sevenoaks News* for 2nd November, 1961, seemed to have been somewhat overcome by the occasion.

It was quite fantastic! Just like V.J. night all over again. Unless you were very determined which way you were going, it was a case of being swept with the tide. The signal box was swamped with visitors, people wandered along the track to reach the extra coaches, and sections of the crowd sang intermittently . . .

A special return trip from Westerham was scheduled at 8.30 pm and was intended to be non-stop to Dunton Green but actually called at Chevening. As the train passed through Brasted station the waiting crowds yelled and screamed their farewells. It really was the end of the well-loved 'Flyer'.

Now, commuters had to accustom themselves to a new routine. Starting on Monday 30th October, 1961, London Transport ran additional buses on route 403: there were five extra journeys from Westerham to Sevenoaks between 6.00 am and 9.00 am, and six extra buses between 5.00 pm and 8.00 pm from Sevenoaks to Westerham. They were planned to give the best possible connections with fast trains at Sevenoaks. What is more, passengers holding season tickets to stations beyond Dunton Green could use the bus route at railway season ticket rates for one year; that is, until 30th October, 1962. After that date, BR effectively disowned the former branch line passengers.

For the casual traveller the 403 bus route was a reasonable substitute for the train, but for the regular commuter, suffering two hard winters in usually unheated 'RT' double-deck buses, it became increasingly unsatisfactory. During the winter of 1962/3 bus timekeeping was poor and connections were missed; often the bus would not turn up at all; and by then each journey was costing the erstwhile season-ticket holder one shilling, or 10 shillings a week for the regular passenger to find. As he waited for the bus at Sevenoaks every evening, getting colder and his nose redder, he thought longingly of the days when travelling on the train to Westerham was a real pleasure after the day's toil in London, something to look forward to. Small wonder that he would do his utmost to get the railway reopened by any means within his power.

Westerham station forecourt was the turning point of Green Line coach route 706 and the rear of an 'RF' coach is visible, right. The fuel tanker had less success turning in the snow of 29th December, 1962, until assisted by WVRA members who spread ashes from the station stove on to the road.   *Alan Snowdon*

Chapter Nine

Efforts to Reopen the Line

The Westerham Branch Railway Passengers Association had been formed in February 1960 to fight for the retention of train services between Dunton Green and Westerham. In November 1961 the Association decided to seek reopening of the line by some independent body. Meanwhile, some railway enthusiasts had formed the Westerham Valley Railway Society, and a census held locally had indicated large support for restoring train services. As the two groups had so much in common, agreement was made to amalgamate them; and in early January 1962 a merger took place, at which four members of the Society's committee were co-opted on to the Association's committee.

A public meeting was held in Westerham on 3rd March, 1962, at which the aims of the Westerham Branch Railway Passengers Association were put forward. The intention was to lease the line from BR and operate an independent train service, using a diesel railcar on Mondays to Fridays for 'commuters' and community, with approximately the same timings and fares as previously obtaining; and a weekend vintage steam train service for enthusiasts, tourists and visitors, running between April and October.

It was reckoned that BR, Kent County Council (KCC) and passengers would all benefit from this service: Southern Region would derive traffic revenue and rent from the line without the cost of operating it, the County Council would receive rates from the line which it would lose if it converted the railway into a road, and passengers would have their necessary rail transport service. Annual rent to BR was assumed to be something in the order of £2,000 per annum, and the minimum 'break-even' traffic receipts needed to be £7,000.

The committee comprised 12 members. Representing 'commuters' were five elected members: Messrs Bentley, J.G. Cameron (secretary), S.F. Curran, W.G. Gray (chairman) and D.E. Walter (treasurer). Seven co-opted members represented the community (Mrs Asselberghs of Brasted, Mr Jenner of Westerham, and Mr F.C. Bryan, a retired telecommunications engineer of Halstead) and railway enthusiasts (Messrs Burkenshaw, R.H. Edwards, D.E. Pope and A.M. Snowdon). Denis Pope acted as railway publicity officer, and the 'enthusiasts' plus Mr Bryan additionally comprised a Technical Sub-Committee charged with considering minimum personnel and rolling stock required to operate the line.

At the meeting Mr Gray (who stressed that he was *not* a railway enthusiast) said the aim was to reopen the line by any means. It was accepted that the railcar service could not itself be profitable; it would be the steam service, run by volunteers as on the Bluebell Railway, that would provide the 'bread and butter'.

From the floor came a query: 'Why use diesel cars? A steam engine you can nurse!'

The committee felt that running railcars was the only economical, indeed practicable, method of providing a serious train service. If a steam engine were used there would be the little matter of paying someone to light the fire at about 4.30 in the morning - an unattractive idea for a company with limited resources.

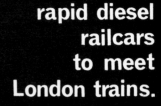

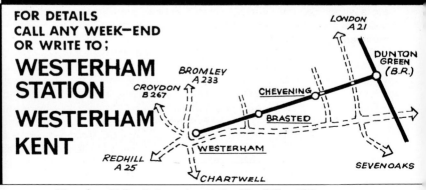
Westerham Valley Railway Association Handbill, *c.* 1963

In reply to other questions the committee stated that Brasted and Chevening Halts would keep open, and that there was no intention of running a freight service. Mention was made of some of Westerham's tourist attractions - Chartwell, General Wolfe and William Pitt - which surely would encourage passengers to use the weekend train service.

The fact that Kent County Council was anxious to convert most of the course of the railway to a road, as part of its great South Orbital Motorway scheme, was known at the time of the March meeting, but it was hoped that somehow the Council could be persuaded to drop the plan if a serious train service were proposed. Throughout the life of the Association this cloud hung around and would not go away; nevertheless in July 1962 the Westerham Branch Railway Passengers Association obtained a lease on the station building at Westerham, which then became its headquarters. Broken glass was replaced, the structure generally smartened up and, for the princely sum of one penny each, members of the public were admitted to the waiting room and platform to inspect the progress. The colours chosen for the overdue repaint of the station building were cream with maroon trim, stated to be the SE&CR colour scheme, and looked very attractive.

Unfortunately another difficulty arose - the British Transport Commission (BTC) was no longer prepared to lease disused branch lines to private operators, as it had done in the case of the Bluebell Railway initially, and now insisted that the Association must purchase the branch outright. Undeterred, despite having very limited funds thanks in part to a low annual subscription of 2s. 6d., the Westerham Railway Association, as it now called itself, offered £30,000 for the line: track, buildings, land, and the branch platform of Dunton Green station. An anonymous backer was prepared to provide the money. Although BR had valued the line at £53,000, it was prepared to sell at this lower price on condition the Westerham Railway ran a commuter service, so that BR could withdraw its annual subsidy to London Transport of £8,700 for the additional buses between Westerham and Sevenoaks. Southern Region announced on 6th September, 1962, that the BTC had agreed to negotiate with the Association.

William Gray, the chairman of the Association, said that a limited company would need to be formed to run the line, and the diesel service would comprise 12 to 15 trains each way, Mondays to Fridays.

By September 1962 there were nearly 600 members of the Association, and a membership campaign was being conducted in the Westerham and Sevenoaks areas supported by posters, brochures and information sheets aimed at residents who were potential users of the line. Roy Edwards was now the membership secretary.

Westerham Valley Railway Association Platform Ticket (c. 1963)

WVRA volunteers clear a pile of earth from the former floor of engine shed in spring 1963, the inspection pit having now been opened up. The trolley was named 'Westerham Enterprise'.

Alan Snowdon

To provide new line wire for the Westerham-Brasted telephone a length of previously-installed 'interruption cable' was recovered. This was of 'plaited' form with six or eight insulated wires. A WVRA member's home-made 'unstranding machine' is seen here in use at Brasted station, 21st September, 1963 (note the pebble sign is still there). *Alan Snowdon*

A private limited company was to be set up by Ian Allan Ltd, the publishing firm, who proposed to operate the line through a management committee on which the WVRA would be represented. This company would then form part of Mr Allan's group of companies. The committee was given a mandate to press ahead with this scheme. At the end of September there were 845 Association members; total income was nearly £151, expenditure nearly £99 and the balance in hand nearly £52.

In February 1963 members received the first of what were to be four issues of *Westerham Flyer*, a magazine published by the Publicity Committee of the WVRA, chaired by David Kitton. In it was a report that a matchboarded corridor Third Brake, SR No. 3554, had been purchased by a member of the main committee (in fact, Roy Edwards) and was currently stored with the intention of offering it for sale to the company destined to operate the Westerham Valley line. Although not revealed at the time, it was located at Hassocks goods yard, and Mr Edwards had bought it for £250.

Sid Beacon, of the Technical Committee, reported that he and Percy Cope had inspected the best two class 'H' tank locomotives, Nos. 31263 and 31518, at Three Bridges on 8th and 9th December, 1962. After footplate rides between Three Bridges and East Grinstead they pronounced both engines as being in very good condition, and Southern Region was willing to sell them for £1,000 each, moreover keeping them in reserve until the Westerham line was purchased.

In the May 1963 *Westerham Flyer* the same two men reported that on 15th March they had visited Ashford Works to inspect the last surviving class 'O1' 0-6-0, No. 31065, which was found to be in good condition, having been overhauled in 1960 and not having worked much since then. This also was offered by BR for £1,000. Class 'C' 0-6-0 No. 31592 was examined on the same day; a WVRA member, R.F. Stephens, had started a fund to preserve this engine with the intention of running it on the line. The locomotive was in excellent condition, and the intention was that if it could be secured by the Wainwright 'C' Class Preservation Society, of which Mr Stephens was secretary, it would run on the line at weekends by arrangement with the Society. When not in use it would live at Brasted as part of a museum open to visitors.

Members of the Technical Committee paid a visit to Worcester to examine five ex-GWR diesel railcars, Nos. 20, 23, 24, 26 and 32, of which it was hoped to purchase three for the proposed 'commuter' service. These cars were single units built in 1940, with driver's cab at each end, and a seating capacity of 48 in an open saloon. All were out of use, in 'reasonable' condition, and were offered for £600 each.

Alan Snowdon made his customary appeal for more volunteers and tools; important work included ditch clearance for good drainage and the oiling of fishplates. BR had agreed to rent Brasted station on the same terms as Westerham, and it was now the base for working parties rather than Westerham.

At a meeting Sid Beacon, the vice-chairman, reported that Mr Gray 'had found it necessary to resign'. Unfortunately this elegant and tactful phrasing disguises a certain amount of behind-the-scenes acrimony, as Roy Edwards revealed to me in 1987:

Negotiations with Ian Allan were conducted by the Association's Chairman, William Gray. When he discovered that Ian Allan was vaguely thinking of converting the line to narrow gauge, either 15 inch or to 3 ft using Isle of Man / County Donegal / West Clare rolling stock, he unilaterally broke off negotiations. When we on the Committee discovered this, we voted him out: the least he could have done was refer Ian Allan's proposals back to us and the Association to decide.

The Association now had to look for another backer to put up the £30,000 required for the line, plus £10,000 for equipment, for Ian Allan had now withdrawn his support since the planning application he had made to develop 'surplus' land at Westerham station for a petrol station had been refused. In 1995 Mr Allan confirmed that he had indeed intended to sell off 'surplus assets' to raise the capital, but after very careful consideration he had concluded that the project was not commercially viable. 'Westerham did not seem likely to be able to generate the traffic necessary even to cover basic costs.'

The *Westerham Flyer* for August 1963 carried the news that an independent company, the Westerham Valley Light Railway Co. Ltd, was about to be formed. Also reported were that an official film was being made of the line by K.C. Tozer, showing the activities of working parties; that a model of sections of the line was under construction by David Perry and others; that a telephone link between Westerham and Brasted stations had been installed; and that Mr C.J. Prescott had been trying out his invention, the 'Railmobile', on the line.

'Prescott's Patent Railmobile' was described as being a railway truck powered by a motor car mounted on it, and was intended to be used on lines closed to normal traffic. Using an end-loading dock, any motor-car could be driven on to the flat platform truck, on which the car's driving wheels engaged with slightly-protruding metal rollers connected by chain to the truck's axle. When the car's engine was started the revolving wheels caused the rollers to turn and thus the odd-looking vehicle was propelled along the track. Mr Prescott had received permission from BR to run his machine, which was in no way connected with the proposed railcar service; when not in use the 'Railmobile' lived in Westerham goods shed. In 1987 Roy Edwards recalled an occasion (1964/5) when Mr S. Colyer, a committee member, loaded a Land Rover on to the Railmobile, roared off up the line from Westerham, pausing briefly at Brasted before continuing to Chevening (where the rails had been removed) and returned to Westerham. 'It was the very last thing to move on the railway.'

At the Annual General Meeting, held in Westerham on 2nd November, 1963, and reported in the final *Westerham Flyer* (dated December 1963), members were given gloomy future prospects. Efforts to raise £40,000 had been unsuccessful, and Kent County Council was about to negotiate with BR to purchase the rail land for a Sevenoaks bypass. The suggestion was made that only part of the line be purchased, and that Westerham station be sold off for development and replaced by an inconvenient halt some way up the line. Thus, the money raised by selling 'surplus' land would be used to obtain part of the railway for running trains, but the proposed railcar service would no longer be feasible and this part of the scheme would have to be abandoned. It was hoped that BR would sell the line for £35,000, without the 'liability' (so-described) of running a commuter service. Only K.C. Tozer spoke out against this new plan. Mr Tozer said it was now a question of running a commuter service or nothing; Kent County Council would have to stand aside. 'The commuter service would not fully cover its cost, but we should be prepared to subsidise it in order to ensure that we could get the line.' This swung the meeting in favour of reopening the line on the original plan.

Acquisition of the line by the Association very nearly happened. In November 1963 another backer was found, terms were agreed with British Railways for the line's purchase and BR wrote that although they were aware of Kent County Council's interest they would not negotiate with that council. Just one month later BR was informed by KCC that sale of the line to them would save Kent's ratepayers £120,000 and, if BR would not sell, it would seek compulsory purchase powers. So Southern Region broke off negotiations with the Westerham people and agreed to sell the line to the Council instead.

The Council's view that filling in the cutting at Chevening, where the Sevenoaks bypass was to cross, was cheaper than bridging the line. Independent engineers, however, considered that the railway route was most unsuitable for conversion into the South Orbital Motorway because of the need to enlarge the earthworks, as well as the risk of flooding. The Council merely stated it had bought the line 'in the hope that the Ministry of Transport might wish to use it'. The route of this motorway had in any case not yet been fixed.

Kent County Council stated that the WVRA might still operate the line on condition it paid for the cost of the bridge, estimated by the County Surveyor in April 1964 as £14,000. It agreed to rent the line to the Association for £3,000 per annum, with the possibility of a reduction to £750 if surplus land were sold. Westerham Valley Light Railway Co. Ltd agreed to all these terms.

In August 1964 KCC informed the railway that its original estimate had been wrong and that it now required £26,215 for the bridge, to be paid in full by 24th August, otherwise the council would instruct its contractors to start filling in the cutting at Chevening. The company was unable to pay this enormous sum, and put forward its problems in the *Kent Messenger* for 14th August, 1964, in an article based on information supplied by the chairman, K.C. Tozer. 'All the company is seeking is fair play.'

Meanwhile, three ex-Metropolitan Railway 'Dreadnought' coaches had been purchased from London Transport by David Kitton: a seven-compartment Brake Third, a nine-compartment Third and a seven-compartment First. It had been planned to work these coaches down from Neasden to Dunton Green by way of Baker Street, Liverpool Street, Aldgate, New Cross and Hither Green, where the Southern 'Continental' Brake Third would be attached, on Sunday 23rd August, 1964. Initially, Southern Region had agreed to allow the Association to store the stock in Dunton Green goods yard for £1 per vehicle per week, but then stated it was 'reluctant' to do so, owing to the WVRA's difficulties with KCC. Class 'H' 0-4-4 tank locomotive No. 31263 had been paid for, and was still at Three Bridges; BR was now in the position of refusing to allow the Association to store its stock at an alternative site, at the same time threatening to scrap the stock if the Association did not take delivery!

By November 1964 arrangements were made with the Kent & East Sussex Railway Society to store the coaches at Robertsbridge for the time being, but in the event they were sent to the Keighley & Worth Valley Railway, the 'Met' coaches on loan for four years and the SR coach being sold. The class 'H' locomotive did go to Robertsbridge, arriving there in a goods train on 17th November. Later its ownership was transferred to a trust to ease the financial burden of the Association. This 'H' Class Trust consisted of four trustees appointed by the committee in 1965.

Roy Edwards, who had purchased his coach in 1962 for resale to, and use by, the Westerham Valley Railway, had offered it to the Bluebell Railway but had received no reply; although he very much wanted it to be kept in the South of England he thought there would never be any other private railways there and so he sold it to the K&WVR for £237 10s. As for the 'Dreadnoughts', these were sold ultimately.

At the November 1964 AGM Mr Tozer reported that the WVLR company had been unable to find the money required for the bridge, but that numerous MPs, concerned about KCC's doubtful methods and reasons for taking over the line, had taken up the Company's case; there was a change of Government in October and there was a faint hope that the new Minister of Transport might prove sympathetic.

Mr Terence Boston, MP for Faversham, sought to persuade the Minister of Transport, Tom Frazer, to intervene and hold an enquiry into KCC's plans to use the railway for its road schemes. The Minister refused, and soon the cutting at Chevening was filled by the road contractors, the track there having been already lifted. With this act all hope of ever reopening the line was killed.

At a Special General Meeting held in autumn 1965 agreement was made to merge with the K&ESR Preservation Society by 41 votes to 7, and to assist in the reopening of the K&ESR by 52 votes to 1. It was felt the best way to salvage something from the wreckage was to seek the preservation of some other line, and the K&ESR was about to be purchased from BR.

In January 1966 Westerham Valley Railway Association members were sent a newsletter stating that, following a vote taken at the AGM on 21st December, 1965, the proposed amalgamation with the Kent & East Sussex Railway Preservation Society was taking place on 1st January, the new organisation being known as the Kent & East Sussex Railway Association.

The Westerham link with the K&ESR did not last long. At Robertsbridge, where their locomotive had been stored in the open since late 1964, Trust members worked on restoration, but No. 31263 never ran on the light railway, which would have needed strengthening in order to permit it. The Trust began to feel that better facilities for work on the locomotive would exist at Ashford, where Mr E. Lewis-Evans had leased the former engine shed from BR; and accordingly No. 263 (original SE&CR number) was moved there on 2nd February, 1969. The Trust's chairman Peter Cox, informed the Association chairman that if the K&ESR ever reopened and invited the Trust to return it would consider doing so.

Ashford running shed, which later became the South Eastern Steam Centre, had several public 'open days' from 1970 to 1976, and passengers could ride in a coach hauled and propelled by the 'H' within the shed limits. However, dissatisfaction set in again, and the Trust wished to be able to run its locomotive on a 'real' railway, rather than shunting up and down for a few dozen yards.

On 24th January, 1976, the engine was taken by road from Ashford to the Bluebell Railway; and there it has remained, an able performer. It was painted in full SE&CR green livery - a declared aim of the Trust from the very start - and is a tangible reminder of the Westerham Valley Railway, upon which it was originally intended to run when purchased from BR.

There was also the 'C' class, No. 31592. As DS 239, this was still in use by BR at Ashford during 1964/5, and was reboiled during this period, not being withdrawn until 1966. Mr R.F. Stephens, who had started the Wainwright 'C' Class Preservation Society in 1962 and was still its secretary, in December 1965 reported that the Society had raised over £1,000 to purchase the locomotive, and needed only another £300, since BR had increased its original price. It was intended that this engine should go to Robertsbridge to join the 'H' there, but in fact it remained at Ashford Shed until 1970.

In February 1970 Mr Lewis-Evans gave the Society six months' notice to quit, and after negotiations with the Bluebell Railway it transferred the locomotive by road to Sheffield Park over the weekend of 15th/16th August, 1970. It was the first of two locomotives originally intended for Westerham that, from 1976, would be stablemates on the Sussex line. SE&CR No. 592, the only surviving locomotive built at Longhedge, had been restored to exact SE&CR condition even before the move, with safety-chains and a lengthened chimney, among other things.

The third locomotive with a 'Westerham' connection was class 'O1' 0-6-0 No. 65, the last survivor of its type. It had been withdrawn in June 1961 and put into store at Ashford; it was reported in the January 1965 *Railway Magazine* as 'awaiting preservation' in August 1964. A member of the Westerham Valley Railway Association was attempting to buy it using a loan from the Association repayable as soon as its commitments allowed. No. 65 was in fact purchased by Esmond Lewis-Evans, and over the next couple of years the engine was put into working order. In 1966 the owner was hoping to find a permanent home for No. 65 and, like the 'C', it was expected to go to the K&ESR around the middle of the year. In October 1968 Mr Lewis-Evans came to an agreement with BR to keep the 'O1' at the former Ashford motive power depot, and from 1970 the public could view the locomotive, and others, on open days at the 'South Eastern Steam Centre'. In 1973 the depot was leased from BR for 20 years, but unfortunately the 'Centre' collapsed in 1976, when BR, claiming non-payment of rent from Mr Lewis-Evans, evicted him on 6th August. Parts of the 'O1', which had been dismantled, were delivered to the Bluebell Railway in June 1997.

Even one of the intended diesel railcars inspected at Worcester in 1963 was saved: GWR No. 20 was acquired by the K&ESR in 1964 and arrived by rail at Robertsbridge on 2nd April, 1966. Because the Hastings line tunnels had tight clearances the car had to be worked as an out-of-gauge load (its body tilted sideways) between Tonbridge and Robertsbridge, no other train being permitted to pass during its journey.

The SR 'matchboard' coach and the three ex-Metropolitan carriages were painted primrose and dark blue shortly after their arrival on the Keighley & Worth Valley Railway in 1965. Ownership of No. 3554 was eventually transferred to the Vintage Carriages Trust and the carriage was repainted in SR fully-lined dark green livery. In 1991 an agreement with the Bluebell was made and the carriage was transferred south for that year's season; however it was still there in 1994, normally working only on peak Sundays.

David Kitton, in a letter to the *Railway Magazine* in November 1965, summed up the whole sad story of the long battle to save the Westerham branch. He considered that the failure of the committee to achieve success provoked much scorn amongst outsiders, but the WVRA *had* secured the purchase price. Kent County Council had then forced BR to sell the line to it instead of the Association. Comparison with other lines was unfair because 'in no case has a line been snatched as success was in sight'. Commenting on KCC's original estimate for the Chevening bridge of £14,000 being increased to £26,215, Kitton remarked: 'In view of this proven lack of estimating ability one speculates as to the reality of the "savings" which KCC used as a lever to gain the line.'

Reflecting back on events, Roy Edwards thought that the disadvantage of the committee was that most of its members were young and inexperienced; there were no 'big names' among them and they carried no clout with the authorities. Although they had friends on BR and some of the committee members were even employed by BR, it was of very little advantage.

The three best-remembered committee members, because they put in not only hours of work behind the scenes but also frequent appearances in working parties at Westerham and Brasted, were Roy Edwards, who later worked in the press office at Waterloo; Alan Snowdon, a jocular individual who used to be in charge of the working parties; and Denis Edward St Kristopher Pope, a 'character' who was thought to have some Russian blood, and who wore a thick moustache; he would turn up at Westerham on his motor-cycle combination which he had named *Hesperus* (although it needed a lot of imagination to see any resemblance between this apparently home-made machine and one of Colonel Stephens' locomotives!). Unfortunately he died at a very young age.

Of the line and its structures, for all the hours of hard work put in, there is practically nothing to show. The track was lifted, Westerham signal cabin was demolished and by March 1966 the station building was gone; the water tower, yard crane and goods shed went very soon afterwards. Brasted station lasted longer but in July 1977 the building was found to have been partly destroyed and in imminent danger of collapse. The former station master's house was still standing in 1995. Most of the trackbed has been obliterated by the M25, and no doubt the officials of the Ministry of Transport and of Kent County Council were all highly delighted at their easy victory over the bold little men of Westerham.

Epilogue

For several years after the demolition of Westerham station the only remnants were the brick base of the station building, the platform (complete with its holly tree), much iron fencing, and the granite setts in the goods yard and station forecourt. Although hardly a traffic objective this forecourt continued to be used by Green Line coaches on route 706 turning here; this hourly service (Westerham-Victoria-Aylesbury) had begun on 26th June, 1946, but ran for the last time on 1st April, 1977.

Now, the town has demonstrated how little it misses the railway by allowing the building of a light industrial estate on the station site, so that even the last few remnants have disappeared; it has seen fit to name the new road that runs through the estate 'The Flyers Way'. All that survived in 1995 was the stump of the goods yard crane, left *in situ* either as a curiosity to excite the attention of future industrial archaeologists, or perhaps because it was so firmly embedded that no one could remove it. Also vanished is an establishment much associated with the railway - the Crown - the endorsement by Gibson Thompson back in the 1890s of its comforts having, apparently, carried little weight in the 1980s.

The Westerham Valley Railway took 17 years to build, from the passing of the original Act to its opening. Its line of route, not particularly well planned, provided a somewhat indirect journey to London. It lasted only 80 years, during the last 30 of which it, like so many other rural railways that did not go where people wanted to go, was much troubled by bus competition. Finally, it was defeated by the powers of both the Government and the local council, both of which seemed to believe that building roads - in a vain attempt to accommodate an increasing number of motor cars and lorries - was more important than almost anything else in the world. The railway may have spoiled the Vale of Holmesdale, as the *Sevenoaks Chronicle* in 1881 believed it had, but the M25 - and particularly the interchange between Chevening and Dunton Green - has surely perpetrated far, far greater damage to the landscape. Few other closed branch lines, especially one that could have had such a great future if the aims of the Association had been realised, can have been obliterated more completely than the unfortunate Westerham Valley Railway.

Brasted station building from the south, 18th April, 1965, partially repainted by the WVRA but now showing signs of neglect. Demolition came about in 1977. *Author*

Index

Acts of Parliament, 8, 11, 12, 41, 61.
Aerial ropeway, 67, 73.
Air raid, 85.
Allan, Ian, 121, 122.
Barton, W.W., 43.
Blackout, 85, 89.
Board of Trade, 13, 15, 41.
Brady, Francis, 11, 12, 13.
Brasted, 8, 19, 27, 41, 44, 84, 99.
Breweries, 43, 45.
Bridges, 15, 19, 27, 40, 54, 102.
British Transport Commission, 97, 119.
Bus services, 10, 44, 45, 81, 85, 99, 116, 127.
Byng, James, 10, 11.
Carriages, 5, 47, 49, 51, 53, 54, 55, 56, 57, 60, 63, 69, 115, 121, 123, 125.
Casserley, H.C., 67.
Chambers, Charles, 12, 13, 41.
Chevening, 19, 53, 83, 102, 111, 123.
Chipstead, 19, 53, 83
Churchill, Winston, 60.
Colyer, Stan, 122.
Combe Bank, 19, 53.
Dunton Green, 19, 42, 54, 56, 67, 84.
Durtnell, Richard, 9, 12.
Dye, E., 9, 43.
Edwards, Roy, 6, 117, 119, 121, 124, 126.
Electrification, 57, 73, 101.
Fares, 18, 43, 61, 75, 81, 97, 111.
Faulkner, F.D.Y., 99.
Fenton, Myles, 17, 41.
Fox, W., 9, 12, 17.
Goods traffic, 43, 45, 60, 81, 87.
Gray, W.G., 117, 119, 121, 122.
Grover, J.W., 9, 10, 11, 12.
Gurney-Smith, E.A., 77.
Hill, Vincent, 48.
Horton, B., 27, 45.
Hutchinson, C.S., 13, 15.
Kidner, R.W., 6, 67, 79, 83.
Kitchen, Joseph, 9, 10.
Kitton, David H., 121, 123, 126.
Knatchbull-Hugessen, E.H., 10, 11, 12, 13.
Locomotives:
  Contractor's, 41.
  '118' 2-4-0, 44.
  'B', 'B1' 4-4-0, 63, 67.
  'D1/M' 0-4-2T, 77.

Locomotives (continued):
  'O', 'O1' 0-6-0, 47, 63, 67, 103, 121, 125.
  'Q', 'Q1' 0-4-4T, 47, 55, 56, 61.
  'Q1' 0-6-0, 115.
  'C' 0-6-0, 121, 125.
  'D1' 4-4-0, 102, 115.
  'M7' 0-4-4T, 107.
  'H' 0-4-4T, 5, 73, 95, 105, 115, 121, 123, 124.
  'P' 0-6-0T, 55.
  'R', 'R1' 0-4-4T, 55, 73, 76, 79, 89, 95.
  'WC' 4-6-2, 102.
Locomotive workings, 47, 55, 57, 63, 90, 91, 95, 101.
Lucas & Aird, 11.
Marples, Ernest, 109, 111.
Mechanical horse, 89.
Pope, Denis, 117, 126.
Populations:
  Brasted, 75.
  Westerham, 7, 18, 57, 75, 99.
Push-and-pull trains, 69, 71, 73, 76, 105.
Railcars, steam:
  Kitson, 49, 51, 54, 76.
  Peebles, 49.
  Sentinel, 77, 79.
Railmobile, 122.
Rodgers, John, 111, 115.
Russell, Ivan P., 103.
Serpell, David, 115.
Shaw, John, 12, 17, 41.
Sheath, Charles, 11, 12.
Signals, 85, 89.
Snowdon, Alan M., 5, 6, 117, 121, 126.
Special trains, 17, 77, 102, 103.
Stanhope, James, 7th Earl, 83.
Station masters, 44, 56, 67, 89.
Stephens, R.F., 121, 125.
Structures, 13, 19, 27, 40, 61, 126.
Sundridge, 19, 42.
Thompson, C.R., 9, 12, 13, 17.
Tipping, William, 8, 9, 10, 12, 13, 41, 44, 45.
Tonge, W.J., 10, 12.
Tozer, K.C., 122, 123, 124.
Train services, 18, 42, 47, 49, 53, 54, 57, 65, 69, 71, 76, 79, 87, 102.
Warde, Charles A. Madan, 7, 12, 13, 44.
Watkin, Edward William, 9, 10, 11, 12, 13, 17.
Weather, 13, 40, 67, 85, 103.
Wreford, Samuel, 42.

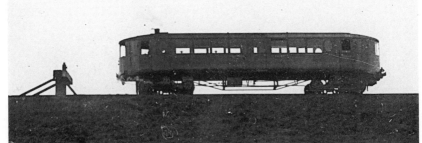

Sentinel railbus No. 6 laying-over on the headshunt at Dunton Green while on evening duty, 28th March, 1936. *R.W. Kidner*